8-2016   10-2019
38m
@15 RV1322
  20

11-09
9m @
avg@15
00/322

Fort Worth & Tarrant County

A Historical Guide

Fort Worth & Tarrant County

A Historical Guide

Edited and Revised by
RUBY SCHMIDT

A Project of the
TARRANT COUNTY HISTORICAL SOCIETY

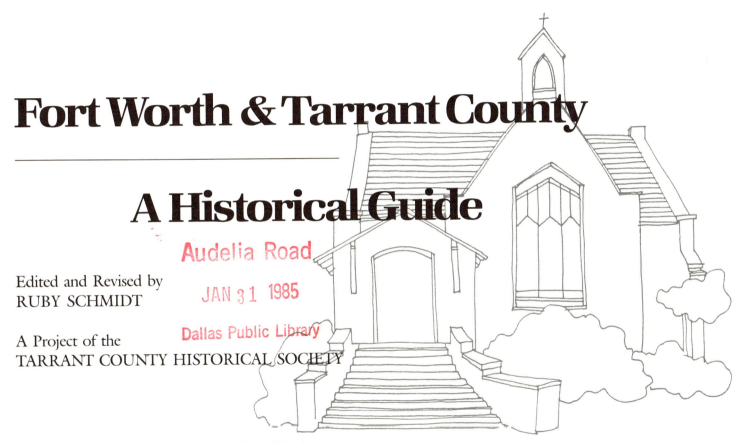

Texas Christian University Press • Fort Worth

Library of Congress Cataloging in Publication Data

Main entry under title:
Fort Worth and Tarrant County.
   Includes index.
   1. Historic sites—Texas—Fort Worth—Guide-books.
2. Historic sites—Texas—Tarrant County—Guide-books.
3. Fort Worth (Tex.)—Buildings—Guide-books. 4. Tarrant County (Tex.)—History, Local. 5. Fort Worth (Tex.)—Biography. 6. Tarrant County (Tex.)—Biography.
I. Schmidt, Ruby. II. Tarrant County Historical Society.
F394.F7F59 1984   917.64′531046   84-90

Copyright © 1984 by *Tarrant County Historical Society, Fort Worth, Texas*
All Rights Reserved
Printed in the United States of America

ISBN 0-912646-93-4 (*cloth*)
ISBN 0-912646-87-X (*paper*)

Designed by WHITEHEAD & WHITEHEAD
Maps and illustrations by JONE BERGQUIST

CONTENTS

Tarrant County History—A Wild & Woolly Past   *vii*
Capsule History of Tarrant County   *ix*
How To Use This Book   *xi*
  1. The Founding of Tarrant County and Camp Worth   *1*
  2. Sundance Square   *5*
  3. Fort Worth—Downtown   *9*
  4. The Stockyards Historical District   *27*
  5. Fort Worth—North Side   *31*
  6. The Cultural District   *35*
  7. Fort Worth—West Side   *39*
  8. Fort Worth—South Side   *43*
  9. Fort Worth—East Side   *48*
  10. Suburban Communities & Unincorporated Areas   *51*
  11. Historic Cemeteries in Tarrant County   *61*
  12. Historic Homes in Tarrant County   *75*
  13. Historic Houses of Worship   *83*
Acknowledgments   *90*
Index   *91*

MAPS

Tarrant County   *xii*
Fort Worth—Downtown—North   *4*
Fort Worth—Downtown—South   *10*
The Stockyards Historical District—North Side   *26*
The Cultural District   *34*
Fort Worth—South Side   *42*
Historic Cemeteries   *60*

The present measures the future by the past.

Tarrant County History
A Wild & Woolly Past

TARRANT COUNTY'S MAJOR CITY, Fort Worth, has been likened to a young hellion who has matured into an unwonted respectability. Where other frontier towns dried into dust and blew away, Fort Worth dug in and survived. In three generations, the remote army post on the Trinity River grew into a major city, its growth paralleling major phases and developments in the American West. And with Fort Worth, Tarrant County grew and prospered, their histories intertwined, their characters identical.

Settled in the 1840s, Tarrant County got its first large influx of population following the Civil War, when Confederate veterans left their homeland to seek their fortunes in the West. Many got as far as Tarrant County and stayed. Next came the famous cattle drives, up from South Texas to the Chisholm Trail in Oklahoma and on to the railheads in Kansas. The drives brought business to Tarrant County, where Fort Worth was the last place for cowboys to have a good time before the long trip north and the last place to stock up on supplies. It was also the first place they hit, with money jingling in their pockets, on the return trip. (To learn more about the cattle drives, please see the entry for Eastern Cattle Trail, Fort Worth—Downtown.)

Then came the railroads—and a real boom period for Tarrant County, as fortune seekers poured into the area by the thousands, setting up businesses, catering to the markets to the west, and making of Fort Worth one of the wildest towns of the West. (Please see entries for Railroads and Sundance Square, Fort Worth—Downtown.)

Finally, in the twentieth century, Tarrant County and Fort Worth owe their continued growth to three industries: livestock, oil and aviation.

Always prominent in the livestock industry, the city became a major livestock center in 1902 when two major packing companies established plants on the North Side. (Please see entry for Stockyards Historical District.) Oil was discovered in West Texas in 1917 and brought another boom that lasted until the Depression. Oil businesses and oil money poured into Fort Worth, the gateway to

West Texas oil. (Please see entry for The Westbrook Hotel, Fort Worth—Downtown.) Aviation came with World War I. During World War II the burgeoning new industry made Fort Worth a center of another kind, with training fields, production plants, and finally, the world's largest airport in the 1970s. (Please see entry for Amon Carter Field, Fort Worth—East Side; related entries are indicated.)

Cattle, railroads, oil, aviation—these form the rich tradition of Tarrant County history, a tradition enlivened by adventures and episodes, some wild, some heroic, some a little funny. There's the story of Hell's Half Acre, a wide open section of town which once was home to Butch Cassidy and the Sundance Kid (please see entry for Sundance Square) . . . and there's the famous gunfight between Longhair Jim Courtright and Luke Short (please see entry for Sundance Square) . . . the Spring Palace Fire with its hero, Al Hayne (separate entry, Fort Worth—Downtown) . . . or the great Southside Fire of 1909 (see Railroads, Fort Worth—Downtown). And then there are the men and women who give history its color and personality, settlers like K. M. Van Zandt, pioneer banker and civic leader, B. B. Paddock, the newspaper editor who crusaded for a fire department, sanitary system and other improvements, Quanah Parker, the last of the Comanche war chiefs who nearly lost his life not in battle but in a Fort Worth hotel room (see entry for The Westbrook Hotel, Fort Worth—Downtown,) and Amon Carter, twentieth century civic leader who among his many accomplishments brought the aviation industry to Fort Worth. (Please see entry for The Cultural District.)

These stories are all told in the pages of this guide to historic sites. The places you will visit with this guidebook in hand are only as important as the people behind them, the people who created the history of this county. So wander through Tarrant County, feel the presence of its wild and woolly past, the excitement of its future, the pride that its people feel in their county.

THISTLE HILL

Capsule History of Tarrant County

1841	Jonathan Bird established Bird's Fort on the Trinity River, south of present Birdville.
1849	Major Ripley Arnold, U.S. Second Dragoons, founded Camp Worth on the Trinity banks; later moved to bluff top.
1856	First stageline brought U.S. Mail on July 18; Fort Worth chosen county seat by bitterly contested election.
1873	Dr. W.P. Burts elected first mayor of Fort Worth when corporate charter was issued for the city; Indian raid near Azle, last in the county.
1874	First telegraph line, Fort Worth to Dallas.
1876	First train from Dallas; first rail shipment of buffalo hides; mule-drawn streetcars between courthouse square and depot at Christmastime.
1877	First phone, between the home of Dr. W.B. Brooks and the drugstore.
1878	First artificial gas manufactured for lighting.
1881	First long distance telephone call, to Dallas.
1882	First public schools opened.
1884	First home delivery of mail.
1885	First electric lights.
1889	Spring Palace, community attraction, opened in May; burned at end of second season in 1890.
1896	First Fat Stock Show, under trees by Marine Creek on the North Side.
1902	Packing houses established.
1903	First car on city streets; first movie, *The Great Train Robbery*.
1905	Theodore Roosevelt here, first president to visit Fort Worth.
1909	North Side annexed.

1911 First airplane landed.

1917 Oil boom began; Camp Bowie opened to train troops for World War I; U.S. aviators began training at three air fields taken over from Canada.

1918 Saloons closed because of prohibition.

1925 First airmail arrived; city manager form of government adopted.

1936 Original Casa Mañana opened at Frontier Days to salute Texas Centennial.

1941 Consolidated Vultee Aircraft opened bomber plant (now General Dynamics).

1942 Tarrant Field Airdrome opened as Army Air Training Center (renamed Carswell when taken over by Air Force in 1948).

1958 New Casa Mañana opened.

1963 First grade integrated by public schools in compliance with court order; President John F. Kennedy spoke here just before he was assassinated in Dallas.

1969 Alan Bean became first Fort Worther to walk on the moon.

1971 Swift and Company closed, ending packing house era.

1973 D/FW International Airport opened.

1981 Sundance Square opened.

ORIG. SWIFT PREMIUM GATE

How To Use This Book

HISTORIC LOCATIONS in this book are arranged alphabetically by city, with some exceptions. Historic sites relating to the founding of the county and Fort Worth are indicated in the early narrative section describing settlement of the area. Three major areas in Fort Worth—Sundance Square, The Cultural District, and The Stockyards Historical District—are listed separately because they contain within their boundaries several sites of interest. Following that, Fort Worth, being by far the largest city, is listed first, out of alphabetical order, and is divided into five sections: Downtown, North Side, West Side, South Side and East Side. Next, cities in the county with historic sites are listed in alphabetical order. Sites in unincorporated areas are listed last.

Because some history buffs are primarily interested in cemeteries, or historic homes, or churches, three separate categories for these sites have been created.

Most but not all sites listed correspond to historical markers. However, information in this guide is not limited to that found on the marker.

For your convenience, names and places in this guide are indexed. In some cases, information about a person or place may be included in the text but not shown in the names of sites listed. In such cases, the person or place will be indicated in the index.

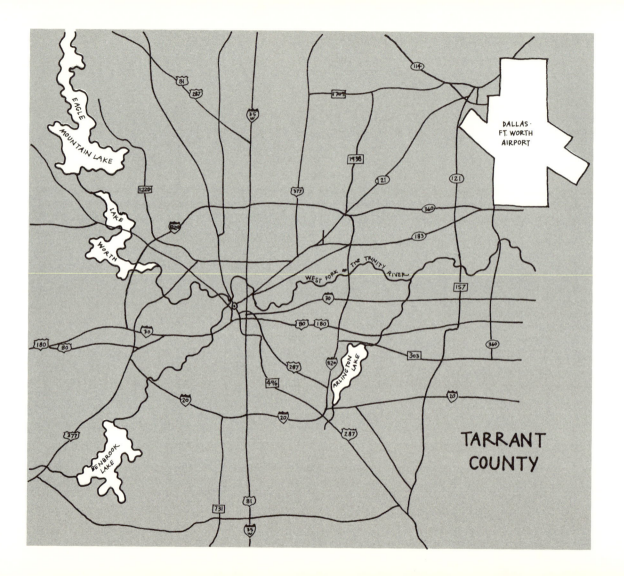

1. The Founding of Tarrant County and Camp Worth

TARRANT COUNTY

Tarrant county was created out of Navarro County in 1849 and named in honor of General Edward H. Tarrant, a well-known Indian fighter. Settlement began in the northeastern corner of the county's 860 square miles which ranged from prairie to rolling, wooded hills. The land included some of the Eastern Cross Timbers, a narrow strip of land between the Northern Blacklands and the Grand Prairie known for its mild climate, good soil, frequent rains, and lush prairie grasses. Indians, primarily Comanche, had occupied the land for generations when the French and Spanish came in the mid seventeenth and eighteenth centuries. The first Anglo-American attempt at settlement came with the establishment of Bird's Fort in 1841. Founded to attract settlers to the area and provide protection from Indian raids, Bird's Fort was established by Jonathan Bird under the authorization of General Tarrant. However, settlers suffered severely from hunger and Indian troubles and soon returned to their former home in the Red River area.

In 1843, troops of the Jacob Snively Expedition disbanded at Bird's Fort after being disarmed by U.S troops. The expedition had been formed to capture Mexican gold wagons on the Santa Fe Trail in retaliation for Mexican raids on San Antonio.

At about the same time, generals Tarrant and George W. Terrell chose the abandoned fort as the site of their negotiations with leaders of nine Indian tribes. The meetings resulted in the signing of the Bird's Fort treaty on September 29, 1843. The treaty called for an end to conflict and the establishment of a line separating Indian lands from territory open for colonization. This line gave Fort Worth its reputation as the city "Where the West Begins."

Birdville, the community which grew out of Bird's Fort, was the first county seat in Tarrant County but in 1856 it lost a bitterly contested election to Fort Worth.

A historical marker on Farm Road 157, one mile north of the Trinity River, marks the site of Bird's Fort. It states, incorrectly, that the fort was established in 1840. A marker near Grand Prairie, Texas, at 2602 Mayfield (near the entrance to Trader's Village), describes the historical Eastern Cross Timbers. The marker was placed by the Tarrant County Historical Commission.

CAMP WORTH

On June 6, 1849, Major Ripley Arnold led a small detachment of U.S. Dragoons as they made camp at the Forks of the Trinity River on the Texas frontier. The fort established on the Clear Fork of the Trinity, one of eight designed to protect the settlers from Indian attack, was named Camp Worth in honor of General William Jenkins Worth, hero of the war with Mexico and commander of the Department of Texas, who had died only a few days before in San Antonio.

Worth had a distinguished service record. He was wounded during the War of 1812, helped set up defenses during Nat Turner's rebellion in Virginia in 1831, and fought against Indians in several areas. But his fame rests on his service during the War with Mexico from 1846–1848. Worth received a sword of honor from Congress and a promotion to Major General for his bravery at the Battle of Monterrey under General Zachary Taylor. In 1847, he was one of the leaders of the conquest of Mexico City. He died of cholera and was buried at Broadway and Fifth Avenue on what is called Worth Square in New York City. A historic marker in the second floor foyer of the Fort Worth City Council Chamber (1000 Throckmorton) describes the life and career of General Worth.

General Worth had been Ripley Arnold's commanding officer in the Mexican War, and Arnold named the site for Worth without realizing that the officer had just died.

Arnold himself had graduated from West Point at the age of twenty-one in 1838 and fought in the Seminole Indian Wars in Florida. Assigned the duty of building a military post on the upper Trinity, he consulted his friend Middleton Tate Johnson (please see separate entry—Arlington, Oldest School). Johnson suggested the junction of the West and Clear Forks, and Arnold established camp there with forty-one men. The camp later was moved higher up the bluff because of high water and a problem with mosquitos.

Arnold's family joined him at Camp Worth in 1850. His wife, Catherine, was a gracious hostess, entertaining on Fort Worth's first piano. At the time, Arnold's pay was sixty dollars a month, with a four dollar ration for guests. He asked for additional funds to cover the constant expense of entertaining.

Ripley Arnold was assassinated in 1853 at Fort Graham, near Hillsboro, Texas, by one of the men under his command, Dr. Joseph M. Steiner. A deep personality clash, growing out of Arnold's stern military discipline, came to a head when Arnold confined Steiner and another man to quarters for drunkenness. In a confrontation in front of Arnold's family, Steiner shot and killed him. Arnold's body was returned to Fort Worth in 1854 and given the first Masonic burial in the city.

During the 1850s, civilization came to Tarrant County. The last major Indian battle occurred in the late 1850s when Indian Chief Jim Ned, enraged at the encroachment of the white man and the loss of a favorite horse to one of Arnold's scouts, planned an attack on Fort Worth. A hundred men under Chief Feathertail and another hundred under Chief Jim Ned gathered for the battle.

Fortunately, a trapper known as Cockrell (or Hahn in German) warned Arnold who, using the tactic of surprise, overwhelmed and defeated the Indians. Though they were pursued as far as Palo Pinto, many Indians escaped.

Tradition among Cockrell's descendants holds that he saved the life of Chief Jim Ned, who was wounded during the flight. As a token of esteem, Chief Jim Ned became a blood brother to Cockrell, giving him the Indian name of Black Bear. Later Chief Jim Ned occasionally camped on land owned by Cockrell, who is said to have been an auxiliary ranger supplying food for Arnold's men.

A Texas Historic Marker located on a spot along the Trinity River, below the All Church Home at 1424 Summit, is intended to mark the site of the last Indian battle, but some sources contend that the battle actually took place on Pecan Street near the courthouse, the original location of the All Church Home.

By the mid-1850s, the line of frontier settlement had extended westward so rapidly that the defense forts were bypassed, and the military abandoned Camp Worth. Civilians took charge, and the city ultimately began to grow southward from the bluff area and northeastward along Samuels Avenue, parallel to the river. Fort Worth was incorporated as a city in 1873, soon after it had become a favorite rest stop for the cowboys who drove their Longhorns northward along toward the Chisholm Trail. The city's robust atmosphere encouraged many merchants to settle and build businesses in the community.

The founding of Camp Worth and its subsequent growth into the City of Fort Worth is described on a historic marker titled "Where The West Begins" and mounted on a granite boulder on the lawn of the Tarrant County Criminal Courts Building (Houston and Belknap in downtown Fort Worth). The marker indicates the approximate site on the bluff where Arnold's troops made camp. However, the original site has been the subject of much discussion and research.

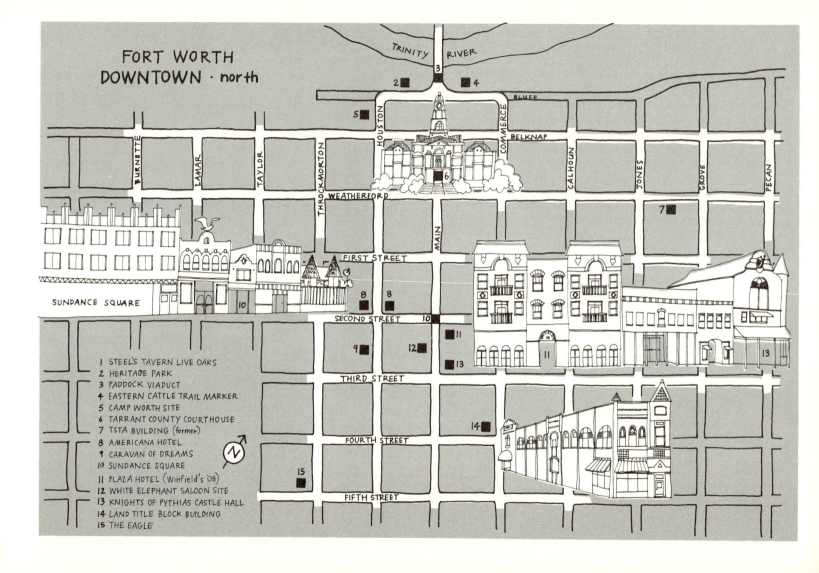

2.

Sundance Square

Throckmorton to Commerce, Second Street to Fourth Street

Sundance square is a collection of turn-of-the-century buildings that have been restored to their original appearance. This two-square-block area along Houston, Main and Commerce between Second and Third streets brings alive an important part of the city's colorful history by recreating the atmosphere of the end of the last century, the days when Fort Worth was a wide open town, throwing out a welcome to cowboys, gunmen, buffalo hunters, and adventurers of all sorts.

Named for The Sundance Kid who, with his partner Butch Cassidy, hid out in Fort Worth, the square echoes the days of "Hell's Half Acre," although that legendary area was south and east of the location of today's Sundance Square. Hell's Half Acre was a fourteen-block area known for entertainment and amusement of a dubious nature. Violence was commonplace as hundreds of fortune seekers swept through Fort Worth in the wake of the great cattle drives, the railroads, and the land speculators. Newspapers carried heartrending stories of suicide among the acre's "fallen angels," and the crucifixion of one, nailed to a wall of an outhouse, horrified local citizens. Laws were passed against guns, gambling and ladies of the night, but money soon stopped flowing into town, and the laws were rescinded.

Butch Cassidy and The Sundance Kid were the most famous of many outlaws who hid in this area. Cassidy, whose legal name was Robert Leroy Parker, was also known as George Leroy Parker and Jim Lowe; The Sundance Kid's legal name was Harry Longbaugh. Around 1898, few realized that the well-dressed Jim Lowe who spent his time in the acre was Butch Cassidy, robber of trains and banks and organizer of the "Wild Bunch." Lowe hid in Fannie Porter's house while posses searched the Northern Plains for him. A photograph made of his gang while they hid out in Fort Worth shows the men dressed in their best suits and wearing derbies.

Etta Place met Butch Cassidy and The Sundance Kid

when she worked in Fannie Porter's house. On February 1, 1902, Sundance and Etta arrived in New York City with a valise containing $30,000 in ill-gotten funds. Etta was treated to Tiffany jewelry and photographed with Sundance before they continued their journey to South America. After five years in South America, Etta returned to this country and entered a Denver hospital for treatment. Sundance and Butch Cassidy are said to have met their deaths in South America, although periodically researchers try to prove that one or the other returned to this country. There are those who say that Etta drifted back to Fort Worth and lived here until her death.

The Jim Courtright-Luke Short gunfight, now a Fort Worth legend, is also connected to Sundance Square. The gunfight took place on Main Street between Second and Third. Courtright, a flamboyant figure who had performed in Wild West shows, served two terms as Fort Worth marshal, then went to New Mexico to work as a guard for a silver mining company. Accused of murder and convinced he would not get a fair trial, he fled to Texas where he established a private detective agency, in spite of the danger of extradition to New Mexico.

One of the most colorful stories about Courtright involves his 1884 escape from Texas Rangers and the Albuquerque Police Chief. Tricked into entering the men's hotel room, Courtright was arrested and placed in jail. Outraged Fort Worth citizens threatened to release him but were calmed by civic leaders who assured them that Fort Worth officers were protecting Courtright and that he was allowed special privileges: He was not confined to a cell, and he was taken to a nearby restaurant for meals. Two days after his arrest, Courtright received word of a plan to help him. At the evening meal, he purposely dropped his napkin and asked one of the guards to pick it up. The guard snarled, "Pick it up yourself!" Courtright leaned down and came up with two guns that had been hung by hooks under the table. Others in the restaurant covered him as he made his escape and mounted a waiting horse.

Courtright escaped successfully and remained in exile for almost two years. Tired of the fugitive role, he returned to New Mexico to face the charges against him and was exonerated. He then returned to Fort Worth where he was given a warm welcome.

Courtright resumed his work as a private detective and discovered that a former friend, Luke Short, had become known as "King of the Gamblers." Short had established the new game of keno at the White Elephant Saloon and Gambling Parlor and customers complained of being "fleeced."

Opinions differ as to what caused the fight between Short and Courtright, but gunfire erupted after a discussion between the two on Main Street between Second and Third. Short stood facing Courtright, his thumbs in the arm holes of his vest. When he lowered his hands, Courtright warned him not to go for his gun. Short denied he had a gun and lifted his vest to show that he did not have a gun under his vest. At this point, Courtright reached for his gun, but Short, having already lowered his hands, fired first with a gun he kept in a special pocket. His shot hit Courtright's right thumb. While Courtright was shifting his gun to his left hand, Short fired again, and Courtright went down. It is said that Courtright, lying in the dust, told Short, "Shoot, Luke, or give up your gun."

Short's reply was "Goodbye, Jim." He shot Courtright again.

Courtright's funeral, from the family residence on Calhoun Street, was the largest held in Fort Worth to that time. Short was "no billed" after a short stay in jail where a threat of mob lynching was dispelled by Bat Masterson, who sat outside the jail with a shotgun.

Luke Short, Jim Courtright, Butch Cassidy, and The Sundance Kid are all long gone from Sundance Square. Today, the historic buildings provide space for offices, restaurants, boutiques, specialty shops, art galleries and a museum. The Sid Richardson Collection of Western Art at 309 Main Street exhibits more than fifty paintings by Frederic Remington and Charles M. Russell from the personal collection of Richardson, a wealthy oilman. The Fort Worth Interpretive Center, located in Fire Station No. 1 at Second and Commerce Streets, provides an introduction to the history of Fort Worth.

Several well-known and historically significant buildings are located in the Square, among them the Plaza Hotel. Today it houses a restaurant, Winfield's '08, named after early Fort Worth cattle baron and oil magnate Winfield Scott (see entries for Oakwood Cemetery, Cemeteries—Fort Worth, and Thistle Hill, Historic Homes—Fort Worth). The City National Bank Building at the corner of Houston and Third, designed and built by Sanguinet and Staats in 1885, has been painstakingly restored. One of the most interesting buildings in the Square is the Knights of Pythias Castle Hall (see following entry). Both the Tarrant County Courthouse and historic Fire Station No. 1 are adjacent to the square.

The Texas Historical Commission in 1983 awarded Bass Brothers Enterprises, Inc., developers of Sundance Square, the prestigious Ruth Lester Award for historic preservation achievements in the square.

Second and Commerce
FIRE STATION NO. 1

In 1873, B. B. Paddock proposed the idea of a volunteer fire department in his *Fort Worth Democrat*. Dr. W. P. Burts, the city's first mayor, donated the site for construction of a city hall which also served as a fire station. A hand-drawn pumper was purchased for $600, and rubber buckets replaced the earlier leather ones used in firefighting.

When Panther City became a name of pride, (see entry for Railroads, Fort Worth—Downtown) firemen acquired two panther mascots, their way of poking fun at the

SUNDANCE SQUARE

Dallas editorial which said Fort Worth was so quiet that a panther could sleep in the center of town without being disturbed. Later, one of the full-grown panthers, Billy, escaped from his cage, causing panic among the men gathered around the pot-bellied stove for a meeting. As firemen exited everywhere, one burned his hands and legs trying to climb the hot stovepipe.

In the early days of the fire department, large cisterns were used to hold water. There was a 1000-gallon cistern at the courthouse, a 500-gallon one at Second and Rusk and another 500-gallon one where the present Hilton Hotel is located. The latter was discovered during construction of the hotel.

The fire bell, used by the department from 1886 until the end of World War I, sounded at every fire, funeral and special occasion. It is presently located in the Texas Street Central Fire Station.

Fire Station No. 1 has been restored, and the Fort Worth Museum of Science and History has constructed a diorama of Fort Worth history, "The Fort Worth Interpretive Center," on the ground floor.

Third and Main
KNIGHTS OF PYTHIAS CASTLE

KNIGHTS OF PYTHIAS

The cornerstone for the original Knights of Pythias Castle Hall was dedicated on June 6, 1881, by the founder of the order, Justus H. Rathbone. It was the first dedication of a castle hall in this country attended in person by Rathbone. The original hall was later destroyed by fire and the present building, designed by Sanguinet and Staats, was built in 1901. A three-story structure with a vaulted slate roof, it is said to resemble both a medieval guild hall and a north European city hall. A seven-foot knight in armor was made in New York in 1882 to stand guard in a high niche on the front of the building, and in 1983, during the renovation of Sundance Square, a replica of the knight was installed in the niche.

From 1947 until 1952, Stanley T. McBrayer, a printer, used this building to conduct experiments suggested by engineer Grant Ghormley, experiments that led to the first offset printing press. In honor of this achievement, a plaque has been placed on the building by Sigma Delta Chi, the Society of Professional Journalists.

Texas Historic Landmark; listed in the National Register of Historic Places.

3.
Fort Worth—Downtown

209 West Eighth
THE ATELIER BUILDING

BUILT ABOUT 1905, this building takes its name from "atelier," (pronounced "a-tel-*yea*"), the French term for an artist's studio. A brick structure featuring two chimneys with terra cotta ornamentation, the building served as the public library in 1936 and has housed the offices of architects and contractors, a restaurant, and financial institutions including the banking firm of Fort Worth benefactor W. R. Edrington. Texas Historic Landmark, 1980.

411 West Seventh
NEIL P. ANDERSON BUILDING

Anderson, a talented broker, moved to Fort Worth in 1878 and set the pace for cotton trading in the inland markets of the Southwest. Sanguinet and Staats designed this building for the Neil P. Anderson Company which conducted business here until 1939. Seven skylights over the cotton grading room afforded buyers better light for examining the product. The building has recently been restored. Recorded Texas Historic Landmark, 1978; listed in the National Register of Historic Places.

Fourth and Main
BURK BURNETT BUILDING

Built in 1914, this twelve-story red brick and limestone structure has engaged granite columns and a three-story limestone base. The two top stories are limestone with bracketed and crested cornices and elaborate Renaissance Revival detail. The building was named by pioneer rancher and oilman Samuel Burk Burnett who purchased it in 1915 and had offices here. The National Foundation for Historic Preservation now has offices here. Listed in the National Register of Historic Places.

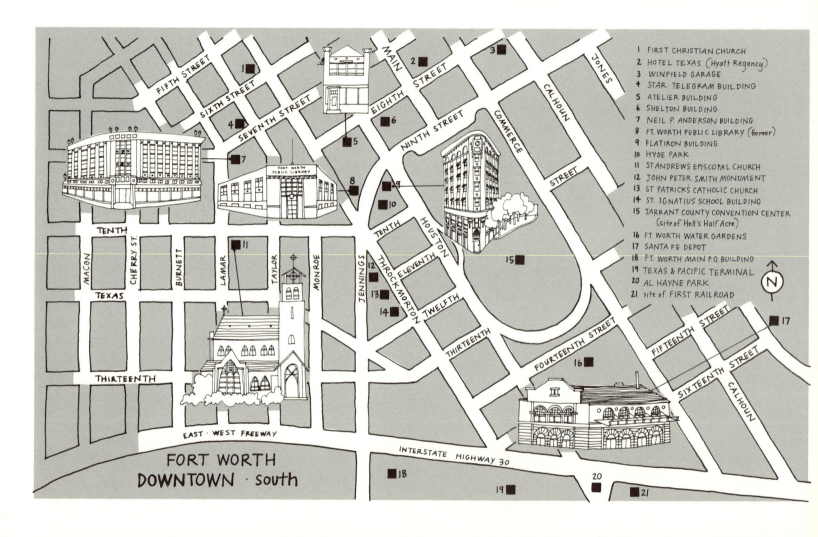

Bounded by Cherry, Seventh, Tenth and Lamar streets
BURNETT PARK

In the early 1900s, Samuel Burk Burnett (please see separate entries for Burk Burnett Building, Fort Worth—Downtown, and Oakwood Cemetery, Fort Worth—North Side) designated this land, slightly over three acres, as a park in honor of his children. He specified that the land was never to be used for any purpose other than a public park. In the 1930s when there was talk of locating a library here, Burnett's heirs objected and would not allow the use of the land to be changed.

In 1983, the Anne Burnett and Charles Tandy Foundation granted five million dollars to redesign the entire park. When completed, the new park will display Henri Matisse's sculpture, *Backs*.

Ninth Street at Throckmorton
CENTRAL LIBRARY

Requesting funds for a public library, local women asked the philanthropist Andrew Carnegie to donate "the price of a good cigar." He responded with $50,000. With that and substantial local gifts, including land donated by Mrs. Sarah J. Jennings, the first city library opened at this site in 1901. The original building was razed in 1938 and replaced with this building in the modern classic style, four times as large as the older building. When the new public library opened in 1978, the property reverted to the Jennings family. It was sold to a private concern in 1982. Texas Historical Marker, 1967.

Throckmorton and Fifth
THE EAGLE, TEXAS AMERICAN BANK/FORT WORTH

The Eagle is one of the major works of Alexander Calder, internationally renowned American artist and sculptor who introduced mobility into sculpture. Calder identified *The Eagle* as a stabile, the term he gave to his non-moving sculptures.

Fort Worth National Bank (now Texas American Bank/Fort Worth) unveiled the sculpture in February 1976, prior to the opening of its new building. The bank is the oldest in Fort Worth, established by Thomas A. Tidball and John B. Wilson, two Confederate veterans, in 1873. Civic leader K. M. Van Zandt soon joined them as a partner, and the bank was active in collecting necessary funds to bring a railroad line to Fort Worth. In 1874, Wilson sold out and a partnership between Van Zandt, John Peter Smith, and J. J. Jarvis, put $22,500 into the bank. Van Zandt was named president. The story is told that once the flooded Trinity River kept Van Zandt from reaching the bank for business, and he threw the keys across the river to a colleague so that business could go on as usual. The bank was chartered as Fort Worth National Bank in the 1880s.

Downtown

East Bluff and Commerce
EASTERN CATTLE TRAIL MARKER

A stone dug from the Trinity River Valley now marks the route of the Eastern Cattle Trail. Cattle were driven north on Rusk Street, now Commerce Street, through the city, down to the bluff and across the Trinity River. Herds rested in the broad valley below the bluff before continuing the long drive north. The stone marking the trail was dedicated on American Heritage Day, July 17, 1964 by the North Star District, Longhorn Council, Boy Scouts of America, Fort Worth.

From the end of the Civil War to the arrival of the railroad in 1876, Fort Worth's economy depended on the great herds of cattle which were driven up the Eastern Trail. The city was the last place for cowboys to stock up on provisions for the trip north as well as the last place they could let loose and enjoy themselves. They spent freely both before the trip and on their way back from the markets.

The Eastern or McCoy Trail joined the Chisholm Trail at the point it reached the Oklahoma boundary and crossed the Red River. Most authorities agree that the Chisholm Trail did not actually extend into Texas. Instead, the state had a series of feeder trails, such as the McCoy, which joined the main trail farther north. Nonetheless, a marker on the east side of Highway 360, near Highway 10, commemorates Jesse Chisholm, the man who laid out the famous trail.

Chisholm, of Scottish and Cherokee descent, was a scout, hunter, trader and trailblazer who spoke about forty Indian dialects and was a respected influence among the Southwestern tribes. He represented the Republic of Texas and President Sam Houston in many negotiations with the Indians, including the 1843 Bird's Fort peace conference (please see separate entry, The Founding of Tarrant County) and the 1849 meetings at Grapevine Springs. The trail Chisholm marked across Oklahoma and Kansas provided a direct route to the cattle markets yet avoided deep river crossings and lay in grassy, well-watered land. Over ten million beeves were driven along the trail between 1866 and 1884. Texas Historic Landmark, 1983.

Tenth Street and Lamar
FEDERAL COURTHOUSE

Designed by architects Wiley Clarkson and Paul Cret, the courthouse was completed in 1933. Two murals, "The Taking of Sam Bass" and "Texas Rangers in Camp," in the fourth floor courtroom were done by Frank Mechau, an artist who was commissioned, during the Depression, to do murals in government and public buildings throughout the country, principally in Colorado.

1000 Houston
FLATIRON BUILDING

Completed in 1907, this seven-story, angular-shaped office building was one of the tallest buildings in North Texas. Designed by Sanguinet and Staats, it stands on a narrow, wedge-shaped lot. The reinforced concrete over steel structure in Renaissance Revival style has a two-story base and a five-story body capped by a cornice with gargoyles and panthers, the latter symbolic of Fort Worth.

FLATIRON BUILDING

It was inspired by similar buildings in Chicago and New York.

Dr. Bacon Saunders, the first Texas doctor to successfully perform an appendectomy, had seen the flatiron buildings in those cities and brought the idea to Fort Worth. Saunders was Dean of Fort Worth Medical College and physician for the Santa Fe Railway.

Texas Historic Landmark, 1968.

Taylor and Bluff
FRENCHMAN'S WELL

Dug high on the bluff overlooking the Trinity River, this well was lined with stone and had a beehive-shaped masonry hood to protect citizens, who were drawing water, from Indians. Tradition claims that a Frenchman named Gounoah built the well, accounting for its name, but other traditions credit it to Louis Wetmore (see entry for Drag Stone, Fort Worth—West Side) and to a man named Barbier.

The well fell into disuse, and, although the Daughters of the American Revolution marked it in the 1930s, it was finally torn down. A token rebirth of the hood on the courthouse square lasted only a short time, because the area was subsequently used for an addition to the courthouse.

The estimated site of the well is just east of Taylor Street and south of Bluff.

South end of Henderson Street Bridge (approximate site)
GRIST MILL AND SAW MILL

Mill owner Julian Feild was one of the first ten settlers in Fort Worth. For a time, he occupied a log cabin formerly used by army officers. When he became seriously ill, a rider was sent to Three Forks (Dallas) to "fetch" Dr. Carroll M. Peak. After successfully treating Feild, Dr. Peak was persuaded to locate in Fort Worth and became the area's first civilian doctor. Feild operated the mill on this spot until the 1850s when uncertainty about the

Downtown

water supply caused him to move the operation to Mansfield. (Please see separate entry, Historic Homes in Tarrant County, the Ralph Man home in Mansfield.)

Commissioned as an officer in the Confederate Army and assigned to milling and delivery of flour and meal, Feild continued after the war to mill and deliver supplies to federal outposts in West Texas, New Mexico and the Indian Territory, using teams of Mexican oxen which allegedly pushed instead of pulling wagons. Several drivers and guards lost their lives in 1873 when Indians, led by Chief Satanta and Chief Big Tree, attacked Feild's freighters. Known as The Warren Wagon-Train Raid, this was the last major Indian attack in North Central Texas.

Feild left Tarrant County for California but returned in the 1870s and in 1886 was appointed postmaster, a position he had held once before in 1856. He subsequently went back to California and died there in September, 1897.

1601 Jones Street
GULF, COLORADO AND SANTA FE DEPOT

Built in 1899, this depot features Beaux Arts design and native stone banding. When intact, the north windows traced travel from the pony express to the steam locomotive. Used by six railroad companies, the depot has welcomed such world figures as Presidents Franklin D. Roosevelt, Dwight D. Eisenhower, and Lyndon B. Johnson. The depot is now used by the Amtrak "Eagle" with service connecting Chicago and Los Angeles.

Texas Historic Landmark, 1970; listed in the National Register of Historic Places.

Bluff and Main
HERITAGE PARK PLAZA

This 112-acre park, located along the bluffs of the Trinity River, was dedicated on April 18, 1980. Hiking and biking trails extend along the river between the Henderson Street bridge on the west and Texas Electric Service dam on the east. The plaza is landscaped with walkways, gardens, waterfalls, ponds, and grottoes.

The Forks of the Trinity can be seen to the northwest from the overlook at the north end of the park. Tradition relates that Robert E. Lee, returning from the Mexican War, looked over the valley from this point and remarked, "I hear the incoming march of thousands of feet."

SANTA FE DEPOT

A metal marker on one of the old liveoak trees on county property, adjacent to Heritage Park, indicates the approximate site of the city's first hotel. Captain E. M. Daggett's lodging house was located in the old cavalry stable of the 2nd U.S. Dragoons. Lawrence W. Steel purchased the property and built a two-story hotel and stagecoach office in 1853.

A marker near the park indicates the approximate site of the first school established in Fort Worth in the mid-1850s by civic leader John Peter Smith. Twelve students enrolled, paying tuition of $5.00 each.

Commerce and Weatherford
HORSE FOUNTAIN

The base is all that remains of this striking drinking fountain, although plans are under way to build a replica. The base of Mineral Wells limestone supported an octagonal shaft of red Pecos sandstone, around which were three water troughs for animals and a drinking fountain. A bronze horse crowned the central shaft. The inscription, from the poetry of Robert Burns, still remains: "Gude masters, a' his weel earned due ye humble beastie gie; Justice 'n mercy's blessings flow nae less for him than ye."

Eighth Street, between Main and Commerce
HYATT REGENCY HOTEL, formerly THE HOTEL TEXAS

The Hotel Texas, designed by Sanguinet & Staats in 1921, was for many years the showplace of Fort Worth hotels. The fifteen-story red brick building with repeated arched windows reveals Chicago, Georgian and Renaissance architectural influences. Its terra cotta ornamentation at street level and at the crest, influenced by Texas tradition, features steer heads as a reminder of Fort Worth's debt to the cattle industry. In 1980, the hotel was thoroughly gutted and renovated into a Hyatt Regency with a soaring atrium, five-story skylight, and a twenty-six-foot cascading waterfall. Careful attention was paid during the renovation to retaining the exterior appearance of the building.

Many important guests have stayed in the hotel over the years. Jack Dempsey signed for the Dempsey-Tunney fight here, and Euday Bowman played his *Twelfth Street Rag* for veterans of World War I. During the Depression, Lawrence Welk led a nine-piece band here. Rudolph Valentino and Aimee Semple McPherson stayed at The Hotel Texas, and on November 21, 1963, President John F. Kennedy spent the night in Suite 850. The following morning he addressed Fort Worth citizens at a breakfast, then spoke to a large crowd in the parking lot across Eighth Street. From there, he flew to Dallas where he was assassinated.

Texas Historic Landmark; listed in the National Register of Historic Places.

Ninth and Throckmorton
HYDE PARK

A young widow, Sarah Hyde Gray (Mason), received a 980-acre land grant from the Republic of Texas in 1836. She married Thomas J. Jennings, who had served as Attorney General of Texas, and later moved to Fort Worth

to oversee the land grant. Sarah Hyde Gray Jennings donated land for this park and named it in honor of her parents, John Hansford Hyde and Polly Stother Gray Hyde.

COMMERCE & FOURTH

LAND TITLE BLOCK BUILDING

Fourth and Commerce
LAND TITLE OFFICE BUILDING

Architects Haggart and Sanguinet designed this brick, sandstone and cast iron building. It features the first known stone carving in Fort Worth, the figures of an owl and mockingbird, and displays the initials of the lawyers, Ross, Head and Ross, who occupied the second floor. With its rounded arched windows and other ornate details, the building is architecturally important because its style was rare in this region in 1889 when it was constructed. Texas Historic Landmark, 1977.

Henderson Street, between Lancaster and Texas
MASONIC TEMPLE

The original ten members of the first Masonic lodge in Fort Worth organized in April, 1854, in Julian Feild's store, with formal chartering in January, 1856. A Masonic hall was erected on the northeast corner of Grove and Belknap, and the first floor was used as a school. The present building is headquarters for four Masonic Lodges and the Shriners. The bell in this building was used in Fort Worth's first hotel and was purchased for the Masons in 1871 by public subscription for use in the school known as The Masonic Institute. It was later transferred to the temple.

301 East Fifth Street
MEDICAL COLLEGE

The Fort Worth Medical College was established in 1894 by a group of prominent area physicians as the Medical Department of Fort Worth University. Its small charter class included Frances Daisy Emery, the first woman medical school graduate in Texas. The college moved to this location in 1905, and in 1911 became affiliated with Texas Christian University. In 1918, the medical college relocated to become a part of Baylor University's Medical School in Dallas. During its twenty-four years in Fort Worth, the medical college graduated approximately 400 students. The building has been razed. Texas Historical Marker, 1983.

Main and Weatherford
MEMORIAL SHAFT

This memorial commemorates Confederate soldiers and their descendants who served in the Spanish-American War, World War I, and World War II. It was placed on Courthouse Square, east of the main entrance to the courthouse, in 1953 by the United Daughters of the Confederacy.

Courthouse Square
PADDOCK PARK

Buckley Boardman Paddock arrived in Fort Worth in 1872 after having served as one of the youngest officers in the Confederate Army. Major Van Zandt hired him to edit the *Democrat*, and Paddock later bought the newspaper. His editorials urged needed improvements for Fort Worth, including a fire department, paved streets, and sanitary improvements. He was a leader in the effort to bring the railroad to Fort Worth, and his concept of a tarantula, with Fort Worth as the body and railroads as the legs, was widely distributed (please see the entry under Railroads, Fort Worth—Downtown). Paddock served both as mayor and a member of the state legislature. A statue of civic leader Charles David Tandy, who died in 1978, was placed in the park in 1981.

Lower level of Heritage Park
PADDOCK VIADUCT

Low-water crossings and ferries originally provided the only access across the Trinity River at this point, connecting the downtown area with northern sections of the city. A two-lane suspension bridge, built in the 1890s, soon proved inadequate for the growing population. This bridge, built in 1914 and designed by the St. Louis firm of Brenneke and Fay, was the first reinforced concrete arch to use self-supporting, reinforcing steel in the nation. Named in honor of B. B. Paddock (see entry above), the bridge has been designated a Texas Historic Civil Engineering Landmark by the American Society of Civil Engineers. Texas Historical Marker, 1980.

Lancaster between Houston and Jennings
POST OFFICE BUILDING

The city's first post office was established in 1856 when Julian Feild was appointed postmaster. Central offices were moved to this building in 1933. Designed by the Fort Worth firm of Wyatt C. Hedrick, it features interior detailing of marble, bronze and gold leaf. Exterior ornamentation reflects the significance of the cattle industry in the development of the city. The massive front columns were not erected in pieces, as was usual, but are solid. Their installation represented an engineering feat for that time. A tablet was placed inside the post office, at the northwest corner, in 1933 by the United Daughters of the Confederacy to commemorate the sixty-eighth anniversary of the reunification of the United States of America. Texas Historical Marker, 1980.

1400 Henderson
PUBLIC MARKET BUILDING

This commercial building was erected in 1930 to provide market space for local farmers, vendors, and retail businesses. It operated until 1941, and the building since has housed a variety of businesses. Spanish Colonial Revival, Italian Baroque Revival and Art Deco styles are evident in the design of the building. Texas Historic Landmark, 1980; listed in the National Register of Historic Places.

Main and Lancaster, southeast corner
RAILROADS

Texas and Pacific Railway Company Engine No. 20 pulled into Fort Worth near this spot on July 19, 1876. In the early 1870s, Fort Worth was financially depressed, in danger of disappearing like other frontier towns. Legend had it that business was so slow in Fort Worth that a panther slept in the middle of one of the city's main streets. When the *Dallas Herald* published the story, the nickname Panther City was applied to Fort Worth. Though the city adopted its new nickname with defiant pride, the tempo of business was slow, and Fort Worth leaders knew the future depended on the railroad's arrival. In 1875, the Texas legislature decreed that its land-grant agreement with the T&P railroad would be abrogated unless the railroad reached Fort Worth by adjournment of the next session.

Tarrant County rose to the challenge and organized the Tarrant County Construction Company. Work began, but progress was slow, and when the legislature announced readiness to adjourn, hope appeared to be lost. Without the railroad, Fort Worth and Tarrant County would never grow.

The drama that brought the T&P to Fort Worth was played on two fronts. In Austin, Tarrant County Representative Nicholas Henry Darnell kept the House in session by his vote against adjournment for fifteen days. Darnell was at the time so ill that he had to be carried on a cot to the House chambers each day, but from his cot, he bellowed "Nay" when adjournment was voted on.

In Fort Worth, orthodox railroad building was abandoned as citizens turned out to work around the clock to complete the roadbed. A crib of lumber and ties, rather than a trestle, spanned Sycamore Creek and from that point on, track was laid on a dirt road, ties weighted with stones. Businessmen sent employees to work on the road, and women brought food and coffee.

On July 19, a huge crowd gathered. Men fired pistols into the air, people cheered and yelled, and the town was wide open for celebration. Railroad Day was by all odds the greatest day in the history of Fort Worth.

The first railroad station, a frame structure, was also located near this intersection. It served as a passenger station, then a freight station, and finally became a section house in 1903.

The Tarrant County Historical Society has placed a plaque commemorating the arrival of the first train on a large column which is now inside the building which stands in the approximate area of the early depot.

The railroad tracks in this area saved Fort Worth in another way several years later when they served as a natural firebreak and stopped the great Southside Fire of April 1909 from destroying the downtown business district. A wholesale, out-of-control fire, this conflagration burned seventeen square blocks and destroyed about 282 buildings, including such major structures as Broadway Baptist Church. The largest fire in the city's history to date, it was started by children playing with matches and fed by unusually strong winds. The Dallas Fire Department, called for help, had nearly reached the scene when they were called back to Dallas to fight fires there.

RAILROADS: *Related Sites*

Gulf, Colorado and Santa Fe Depot—Fort Worth, Downtown
Old 610—Fort Worth, South Side
Texas and Pacific Railroad Terminal Building—Fort Worth, Downtown

901 Houston
THE SHELTON BUILDING

Constructed in 1900, this building first housed a general merchandise establishment, The Daylight Store. In 1910 it was purchased by John M. Shelton, who added a third story and leased the building to S. H. Kress and Company. It was remodeled in 1937 and leased to McCrory's variety store. Texas Historic Landmark, 1980.

1100 Throckmorton
SMITH, JOHN PETER

This marble bust of one of Fort Worth's early settlers was done from a death mask. It is placed near Saint Patrick's Cathedral for which Smith donated the land.

Smith migrated to Fort Worth from Kentucky in 1853 and worked as a teacher, clerk and surveyor. In 1853 he was named Deputy Surveyor of the Denton Land Department and paid in property. A student of the law, he was later admitted to the bar. Although he opposed the secession of Texas during the Civil War, Smith raised a company of Tarrant County men for the Confederacy and joined Sibley's Brigade in 1861. During the war, he served in the unsuccessful invasion of New Mexico and the recapture of Galveston in 1863. He was severely wounded later that year in Louisiana.

Smith returned to Fort Worth after the war and became active in the development of the city. He helped organize a bank, a gas light company, and a street railway and donated land for parks, cemeteries, and hospitals, one of which was later named John Peter Smith Hospital. In 1882, he became mayor of the city. Under his guidance, many public services were established, including the school system and the water department. Smith died in 1901 in St. Louis, Missouri while on a promotional trip for Fort Worth.

Main and Lancaster, south side
SPRING PALACE

Following a suggestion by General R. A. Cameron, an officer of the Fort Worth & Denver Railway, city promoters developed the idea of an annual exhibition for the display of Texas agricultural products. In 1889, they constructed the Texas Spring Palace to house the exhibits. Located south of the present T&P tracks along Vickery Boulevard between Galveston and Jennings avenues, the two-story wooden structure was designed by the Fort Worth firm of Armstrong and Messer and featured Oriental and Moorish details. The outside was a mass of figures and designs made from corn, corn-cobs, husks, and stalks. Each floor was draped with live-oak moss, cotton, the stalks of various grains, and colored grasses peculiar to Texas.

The building was crowded on May 30, 1890, the last night of its second season. As the Elgin National Watch Company band concluded its concert, fire broke out. Moments later, the building was a mass of flames, the sides collapsing inward on the 250-foot main section. Men, women, and children were caught in a crush at the entrances and on the stairways, with some leaping from the second story.

Fortunately, there was only one fatality in the fire. Alfred S. Hayne, an English civil engineer, returned to the burning building to help others trapped inside and saved many lives. He died the next day of burns suffered in the rescue effort and is buried in Oakwood Cemetery.

In 1893, the Women's Humane Association dedicated a watering fountain and monument to his heroism and courage. A local marble cutter, Lloyd Brown, was the original sculptor. In 1934, the bust was repaired and cast in bronze by Fort Worth sculptor Evaline Sellors. Later, when expansion of Main Street required moving the monument, restoration was sponsored by The Fort Worth Art Association.

There was also a heroine of the Spring Palace fire. Ada Large, later Mrs. B. M. Mustard, was given a gold medal for her heroic conduct in saving children from the fire, despite her own burns. She also received $25 in gold.

A reporter from *Frank Leslie's Illustrated Newspaper* who witnessed the fire wrote, "No incident in the recent history of Texas has been more startling . . ." According to the account, the fire began when a boy stepped on a match near the base of a decorated column. The tiny spark thus created ran like a streak of lightning up the column, enveloping the upper floor in less than a hundred seconds.

At the time of the fire, Frank Leslie's special railroad car was standing on the track directly opposite the building, and George E. Burr, chief artist for the journal, made an on-the-spot sketch of the spectacle of the burning building, which was later published.

Efforts to rebuild the Texas Spring Palace failed because of economic problems in the Panic of 1893.

Texas Historical Marker placed in Al Hayne Park, 1980, by the Tarrant County Historical Society.

Downtown

100 Block, Taylor Street (Tandy Center to River Parking Lot)
TANDY CENTER SUBWAY

The world's first privately owned electrical underground subway was the brainchild of brothers Marvin and O. P. Leonard, owners of Leonard's Department Store. Construction and excavation began in 1962. The tunnel, reaching a depth of forty-two feet, had to be blasted through solid rock. More than 9,000 tons of cement were required before a tenth of the project was completed. Over 400 tons of steel were used, and 40,000 tons of earth had to be removed to make the tunnel, which is twenty-one feet wide and fourteen feet high. Underground springs were a constant problem, necessitating a pump and drain system. One spring, which was eighty feet below the surface of the ground, was the probable water source for Frenchman's Well (see separate entry).

Officially named the M & 0 Express at its 1963 opening, the subway used electric cars adapted from earlier use by the Washington, D.C., Transit Company. The cars have recently been modernized. Tandy Center now uses this subway for the public in the same manner as it was first conceived by the Leonard Brothers. Electric cars carry shoppers to and from a fourteen-acre parking lot along the banks of the Trinity River, northwest of the central business district.

1111 Houston
TARRANT COUNTY CONVENTION CENTER

When it was opened in 1968, this complex was the first to house arena, meeting rooms, banquet hall, exhibit hall, and theater under one roof. It covers ten city blocks and has 145,000 square feet of exhibit space, an arena seating 14,000, approximately twenty-five meeting rooms, and a theater seating slightly over 3000. It was also the first building to use closed circuit television for information and security. The Convention Center was enlarged and additional parking facilities, including a covered garage, added in 1983.

Main at Weatherford
TARRANT COUNTY COURTHOUSE

Completed in 1895, the Tarrant County Courthouse cost $408,840 to construct. Citizens of the county were so angered by this extravagant cost that they ousted the county officials responsible.

Built of red granite in a Renaissance Revival style resembling the Texas State Capitol, the four-story building was designed by Gunn and Curtis and built by Probst Construction of Chicago. All materials except the hardware are native to Texas, and the walls at the base of the building are five feet thick. Over the years, the building was remodeled in a haphazard fashion; spacious courtrooms were cut up into offices and dramatic ceilings were lowered. In 1982–83, the courthouse was completely renovated and restored to its original appearance. Recorded Texas Historic Landmark; listed in the National Register of Historic Places.

Second and Houston, northeast corner
TELEPHONE EXCHANGE

A bronze plaque in the sidewalk indicates the site of the first telephone exchange established by Southwestern Telephone and Telegraph Company in Fort Worth in 1881. It initially served forty customers and had three employees. The office was moved in 1895. Marker placed by Southwestern Bell, 1981.

Lancaster at the south end of Throckmorton
TEXAS AND PACIFIC TERMINAL BUILDING

T & P company officials had this passenger terminal constructed in 1931. Designed by Wyatt C. Hedrick, it is Fort Worth's strongest example of the zigzag phase of Art Deco style. The typical exterior ornamentation of geometric and curvilinear lines includes motifs from four periods: Egyptian, Neo-Baroque, American Indian and Gothic. Inside, the building has high ceilings of gold and silver leaf and ornamental plaster, elaborate chandeliers, huge mirrors, metal grills, brass doors on the elevators, bronze entrance doors, and marble floors. The last passenger train stopped at this depot in March, 1967. Texas Historical Marker, 1980; listed in the National Register of Historic Places.

The T & P Warehouse next door also features Art Deco ornamentation, with inlaid panels of white stone and blue tile set in cream-faced brick. The blue and orange zigzag ornamentations on the face of the building are polychromed brick. Mayan motifs grace the sides.

1301 West Seventh
TEXAS AND SOUTHWESTERN CATTLE RAISERS ASSOCIATION

A non-profit organization, TSCRA was formed in 1877 in Graham, Texas, to capture and bring to justice cattle rustlers who were taking advantage of the wide open range. The organization maintains files of all cattle brands and records of all sales and publishes *The Cattleman* magazine. This building is owned by the Texas and Southwestern Cattle Raisers Foundation, a research and educational foundation, which leases this building to the association.

The Cattleman's Museum on the ground floor of this building, open to the public, tells the story of cattle ranches in the Southwest through pictures, displays and video tapes. The Waggoner Library holds the minutes of TSCRA board of directors meetings and the archives of *The Cattleman*. Memorial Hall honors such noted cattle raisers as Samuel Burk Burnett, Cornelia Adair, Charles Goodnight, Captain Richard King, and Captain John Armstrong.

A bronze sculpture, *The Brand Inspector* by Jim Reno, stands in front of the building. It was donated by the Anne Burnett and Charles Tandy Foundation in honor of "those vigilant lawmen cowboys who have tirelessly served the Southwestern cattle industry."

410 East Weatherford
TEXAS STATE TEACHERS ASSOCIATION

This building was constructed in 1930 to serve as the headquarters of the Texas State Teachers Association. Designed by Fort Worth architect Wiley G. Clarkson, it features Renaissance Revival styling. In 1949, TSTA offices moved to Austin. The building was purchased by the Texas and Southwestern Cattle Raisers Association which had its offices here for thirty years before moving to West Seventh. Texas Historic Landmark, 1981.

800 West Seventh at Macon
TURNER & DINGEE GROCERY STORE

Originally called Turner and McClure and located at 502 Houston, the store employed Arthur S. Dingee in 1886. He later purchased the business. As a mark of respect, Dingee retained Turner in the official name of the store even though Turner had died several years before. The store was purchased by Lloyd F. Hallaran in 1923 and moved to this address in 1925. It is still in operation today in the midst of the downtown area and is a popular luncheon sandwich spot for downtown workers. Plaque approved by the Tarrant County Commissioners Court.

810 Houston
W. T. WAGGONER BUILDING

Once the home of the Continental National Bank and later Rattikin Title Company, the twenty-story Waggoner Building was for many years the only skyscraper in Texas west of Dallas. It has been renovated. Listed in the National Register of Historic Places.

Houston and Commerce, from 13th to Lancaster
WATER GARDEN

Given to the citizens of Fort Worth by the Amon G. Carter Foundation, this award-winning water garden features water cascading over multi-tiered ledges, more than 500 trees, and 32,000 horticultural specimens. It was designed by the renowned architectural firm of Philip Johnson and John Burgee and completed in 1974 at a cost of seven million dollars. Sitting on land that was once part of "Hell's Half Acre," (please see entry for Sundance Square, Fort Worth—Downtown), the garden was used for scenes from the movie *Logan's Run* and for a Public Broadcasting Service movie, *The Fort Worth Water Garden*.

1500 Eleventh Avenue
WATER WORKS

Fort Worth's first artesian well was drilled in 1878. Prior to that time, water for domestic use was obtained from shallow wells, springs, or directly from the Trinity River. A great many sewers were merely open ditches which were flushed with water periodically.

The first water works was built in 1888 by a private company. The Holly Plant on this site was completed in 1892 with a pumping capacity of sixteen million gallons per day. A prolonged drouth in 1901 and the disastrous Southside fire of April 3, 1909 indicated a great need for additional water supplies. A dam was completed on the West Fork of the Trinity, creating Lake Worth, in 1914. Eagle Mountain Lake was completed in 1931 and Benbrook Lake in 1949. These lakes provide flood control as well as water supply.

The Holly Plant has been enlarged several times and is still in operation.

Fourth Street, between Houston and Main
THE WESTBROOK HOTEL

This was once the site of the hotel central to Fort Worth's involvement in the oil industry. Like the livestock industry, oil was central to the growth of the city. Oil was found at Ranger, Texas, in 1917 and one after another, wells came up all over West Texas. The three great oil developments—Ranger, Burkburnett, and Desdemona—went full blast through World War II and into peacetime.

A concentration point for oil operators and a center for their frantic transactions, Fort Worth became the gateway to the West Texas oil fields. Oil companies made the city their headquarters. Oil-rich ranchers and farmers moved here. The first skyscrapers were built with oil money—the Life of America, Sinclair and W. T. Waggoner buildings. Refineries added new industry to the city, bringing tremendous increases in payrolls and population.

The Westbrook Hotel was the center of these oil transactions, so crowded that the management was forced to clear the furniture from the lobby. Even so, the crowds spilled over into the street where a board was kept to keep people informed of the latest advances in trading.

A pedestaled statue in the hotel lobby was called The Golden Goddess because she looked down on all these transactions. (Please see also entry for Spaghetti Warehouse, Stockyards Historical District.) Previous to the Westbrook, other hotels had stood on this site, some with interesting stories of their own.

The first, The El Paso, opened in 1877. It had become The Pickwick by December, 1885, when Quanah Parker, the famous Indian chief, nearly lost his life in that hotel. Parker, who had surrendered to reservation life in 1875, acted as a representative to the whites for the Indians who leased land to large ranchers. He was therefore a frequent visitor to Fort Worth, doing business with Samuel Burk Burnett, Tom Waggoner, and others.

On this occasion, he and a friend, Yellow Bear, checked into The Pickwick. Yellow Bear retired early but Parker left the hotel with George W. Briggs, foreman of the Waggoner Ranch. Returning later, Parker, unfamiliar with gas lights, did not shut the valve completely. Gas fumes awakened him during the night but, not realizing the danger, he covered his head and went back to sleep. Both men awakened during the night, feeling ill, then fell unconscious. They were not discovered for thirteen hours. Parker, having fallen near a window, was revived, but Yellow Bear was pronounced dead "by inhalation of gas because someone failed to turn off the gas and blew out the light." Parker requested a copy of the inquest results, fearing his tribesmen would not believe the circumstances.

The hotel became The Delaware in 1891. In 1910, the building was razed, and The Westbrook was built on the site. It was razed in 1978.

Corner, Ninth and Commerce
ZANE-CETTI BUILDING CORNERSTONE

Civil Engineeer J. S. Zane-Cetti, surveyor of Fort Worth's first boundary and much of the Texas & Pacific Railroad right-of-way in West Texas, constructed a stone building on this spot of materials quarried in Austin and hauled here by wagon. Tenants of the building at times included a maker of horse collars and a printing firm. When the structure was razed, a historical marker was erected, incorporating the building's cornerstone and bearing this inscription: "Erected 1889, Cetti and Roche, W. L. Rail Builder."

Zane-Cetti, who also built a brewery on Jones Street between Ninth and Twelfth, constructed his name from his original surname of Zane plus the surname of his stepfather, Cetti.

TARRANT COUNTY COURTHOUSE

Downtown

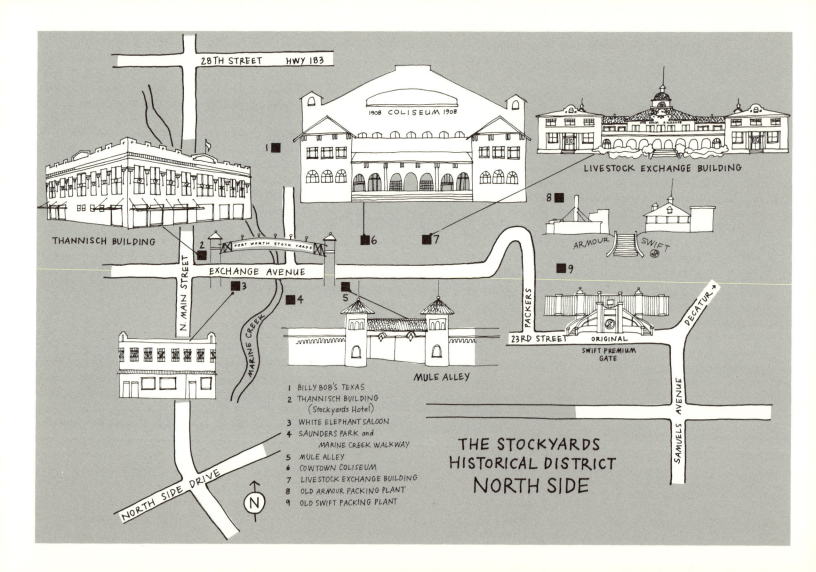

4.

The Stockyards Historical District

THE STOCKYARDS HISTORICAL DISTRICT contains several buildings of special interest and serves as a visual reminder of the importance of the livestock industry to the growth and development of Tarrant County and the City of Fort Worth.

The strong bond between Fort Worth and cattle began in the days when the huge trail drives roared through the city, taking beeves to northern markets. (Please see entry for Eastern Cattle Trail, Fort Worth—Downtown.) The city's history as a livestock market dates back to the 1870s when T. B. Saunders went into business as a cattle buyer. (Please see following entry for Saunders Park.) In 1890, the Fort Worth Dressed Meat and Packing Company built a plant on the city's North Side and several prominent citizens combined to build an associated stockyards.

Fort Worth became a packing house center in 1902 when two major packing companies, Swift and Company and Armour, built plants on the North Side. Within a decade, sixteen million head of stock had passed through the city's stockyards. There were packing plants, cattle pens, barns and sheds and cold storage facilities. Fort Worth had the second largest livestock market in the U.S. and the most modern and extensive horse and mule department in the world. The Fort Worth Belt (Fort Worth Stockyards Belt Railway) was built, with facilities for servicing grain, packing and produce companies.

In 1911, the City of Niles was incorporated. It was named for Louville Veranus Niles, a successful Boston businessman who reorganized the Fort Worth Packing Company in 1899, a move that allowed Swift and Armour to locate their plants here. Extending from 29th Street to Marine Creek and from North Main to one block east of Decatur, its one-and-one-half square miles encompassed the stockyards district, the major meat packing firms, two grain elevators, a cottonseed oil company, a petroleum refinery, and a pipeline plant. By the 1920s, property values in Niles exceeded thirty million dollars and the city was known as the "Richest Little Town in the World." Because of its substantial tax base, Niles was a progressive community with improved roads, utilities, city services and two school districts. Despite legal efforts to avoid annexation, Niles became part of Fort Worth in 1923.

Texas Historic Landmark, 1981; plaque at head of East Exchange Avenue placed by the North Fort Worth Historical Society and the North Fort Worth Businessmen's Association. One of the county's oldest cemeteries is also located within the boundaries of Niles, between the present railroad tracks. Only a few rock markers remain.

123 East Exchange
COWTOWN COLISEUM

Built in 1908 to provide a permanent home for the annual Fat Stock Show, this Mission-style coliseum, 175 feet long and 200 feet wide, was hailed as the largest show arena of its day.

In 1918, the coliseum was the home of the world's first indoor rodeo. Other rodeo innovations have taken place here, such as the introduction of side-release chutes. Over the years, many dignitaries have appeared in the building, including Comanche Chief Quanah Parker (please see separate entry, Westbrook Hotel, Fort Worth—Downtown), Theodore Roosevelt, Enrico Caruso, Bob Wills, Elvis Presley, Harry James, Bob Hope, and Roy Acuff. Billy Sunday held revivals here, Jess Willard fought exhibitions, and Fort Worth youth participated in athletic competitions.

The City of Fort Worth purchased the coliseum in 1936. Since that time, it has been used for a variety of events, including community festivals. Today it is the home of The Cowtown Rodeo, which presents traditional rodeo events every Saturday night during a spring and fall season.

Declared an Archeological Landmark by the Texas Antiquities Commission; listed in the National Register of Historic Places.

131 East Exchange
THE LIVESTOCK EXCHANGE

The Exchange was built in 1903 by the Fort Worth Stockyards Company. Its Spanish-style architecture features a red tile roof, beige stucco walls, and an iron fence enclosing the courtyard. Built to house the Stockyards Company, the Livestock Commission, and the offices of prominent buyers, it once held the offices of forty-two livestock commission companies, the Western Union Office, the Livestock Marketing Association, and the

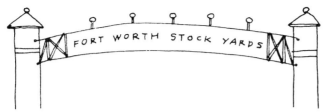

Texas and Southwestern Cattle Raisers Association. The building was purchased in 1944 and completely renovated in 1978. Today, it holds the offices of cattle dealers and the Stockyards Company, along with attorneys, architects, art galleries, and other commercial interests. A Texas Historical Marker for the building is located on the front lawn. A plaque at the east side of the building recognizes the importance of cattle brands in Texas history.

102 East Exchange
THE MAVERICK HOTEL

Built in 1905, the Maverick Hotel provided a lavish headquarters for cattle dealers, cowmen, ranchers and gamblers. Although the building was used for a variety of purposes, including storage, it boasted the county's longest continuously operating bar until the most recent occupant, The Stockyards Social Club, closed its doors in 1982.

South of the 100 Block of East Exchange
SAUNDERS PARK

The Saunders family has been active in the Texas cattle industry since Thomas Bailey Saunders, a North Carolinian, started a cattle ranch near Gonzales. After the Civil War, Bailey drove cattle to both New Orleans and Kansas. He eventually settled in Bexar county.

Two of his eleven children continued the family cattle tradition. William David Harris Saunders supplied beef to the Confederacy and later settled in Goliad as a merchant and rancher. George Washington Saunders was a well-known trail driver of the 1870s. He later opened a livestock commission in San Antonio and helped to organize that city's Union Stockyards.

Thomas B. Saunders II moved to Fort Worth in 1900 and became the first cattle dealer in the local stockyards. He was a pioneer in the use of trucks to transport cattle. During the Depression, his son, Thomas B. Saunders III, established a cattle clearinghouse to provide markets for area livestock.

The stream running through the park is known as Marine Creek. In the late 1890s, the forerunners of the Southwestern Exposition and Fat Stock Show were held on the banks of this creek when cattlemen organized impromptu competitions. Marine Creek, which flooded often and badly, was landscaped in the late 1970s as a flood control and beautification project.

This park was dedicated in honor of the Saunders family, many of whom still live in Tarrant County, in 1981. Texas Historical Marker, by the North Fort Worth Historical Society.

Exchange and Packers Avenue
SPAGHETTI WAREHOUSE

This building was used for seventy-five years as the offices of Swift and Company. Tiny octagonal tiles in the floor bear the Swift emblem.

Today, it serves as a restaurant full of relics of the past. Twelve matching stained glass windows have replaced the original windows, complementing the genuine Tiffany garden scene inside. The bar in the restaurant was brought here from Manitou Springs, Colorado, and the glass-topped elevator which now seats patrons once carried Prime Minister Churchill and General Eisenhower to the British War Office. An old Dallas streetcar holds several tables, and the Golden Goddess from the Westbrook Hotel (please see separate entry, Fort Worth—Downtown) presides over all.

LIVESTOCK INDUSTRY: *Related Sites*

Eastern Cattle Trail Marker, Fort Worth—Downtown
Jesse Chisholm, Founder of the Chisholm Trail—please see Eastern Cattle Trail Marker, Fort Worth—Downtown
Texas and Southwestern Cattle Raisers Association, Fort Worth—Downtown

Stockyards District

5.

Fort Worth—North Side

Samuels Avenue and Cold Springs Road
ARNOLD PARK

This park is located in the area of the cold springs where Major Arnold and his army unit stayed on their way to the site of Camp Worth. The springs, now not identified, are sometimes referred to as Terry Springs in honor of a former landowner.

Arnold Park stands on the site of a house bought by the county for an orphanage. During Fort Worth's wide open days, Mrs. Belle Burchill and another woman, Delia Collins, frequently assisted a Methodist minister on errands of mercy in Hell's Half Acre. In 1887, Mrs. Burchill, with the help of the Tarrant County Commissioners, converted the house on this spot, a former house of ill repute, into an orphanage which housed many children who came from Hell's Half Acre. The home was later incorporated as the Fort Worth Benevolent Home Association and moved to another site.

108 Northeast 28th Street
BRUMBAUGH'S FURNITURE

The mural on the exterior wall of this building, depicting cattlemen in action, was designed and executed by Dennis Blagg and Jim Malone from action shots taken at Texas ranches. The actual painting was done by Wes and Jerry Badgero. Although independently done in the early 1980s, these murals complement the "Painted Spaces" seen on the exterior of several downtown buildings.

Samuels and Pavilion
GRUNEWALD PAVILION AND AMUSEMENT PARK

From 1885 until 1905, Peter Grunewald operated a dance hall and park in this area. Fort Worth lodges and organizations rented the hall which had shuttered windows, seats around an oval floor, and a saloon in the basement. As business declined, the pavilion was closed. The building was later razed and the material used to erect houses on Samuels Avenue. The basement saloon was filled with sand and planted as a peach orchard.

The first camp of settler Ed Terrell was located somewhere between the site of the pavilion and Trader's Oak (please see separate entry, this section). Terrell and a companion, John R. Lusk, camped here in the early 1840s, but were captured by Indians. Terrell managed to escape by tricking the Indians, telling them he needed more flour to make biscuits for them. He fled to East Texas and did not return to Tarrant County for several years.

North bank of the Trinity River, west of Main
(Present site of the TESCO Plant)
HERMANN VEREIN (SOCIETY) PARK

Two acres north of the bluff were established as a park in the late 1890s by a committee from the Order of Sons of Hermann Lodges. Primarily used by the German population of Fort Worth, the park hosted social functions such as the Mai Fest. Dancing, pinochle, visiting, and German meals were the principal interests of the society. The park was closed by 1922 when Texas Electric Service built its power plant.

1012 North Main
KU KLUX KLAN BUILDING (now Ellis Pecan Company)

This building was constructed as a meeting place for the Ku Klux Klan. The Klan, which paraded openly on Civil War anniversaries, was so strong in the early 1920s that it was believed a politician could not be elected without the organization's backing. In 1922, about 5,000 hooded klansmen paraded silently through the city's darkened business district carrying flaming crosses. After this building was damaged by fire, the local klan lost strength. The Klan in Texas disappeared when Governor Ma Ferguson passed a law forbidding concealed faces at public meetings.

700 North Calhoun
LA GRAVE FIELD

Home of the popular Fort Worth Panthers or Cats of Texas League Baseball during the 1920s and 30s, this field was later used as a training ground for young players and a pasture for old ones. The Texas League disbanded temporarily during World War II, but after that, the Panthers played until the team dissolved in the 1950s.

North Main, six miles north of downtown Fort Worth
MEACHAM FIELD

Originally called Fort Worth Airport, Meacham Field was established in 1925 and its name changed, in 1927, to honor former mayor of Fort Worth, Henry C. Meacham. The first airmail plane landed here in 1926, and in 1927 Charles Lindbergh landed at the airport. Wiley Post and Will Rogers were frequent visitors. In 1929, Reg Robbins flew out of Meacham Field to stay aloft 172 hours and thirty minutes, setting a new endurance record.

Texas Air Transport, founded here by Alva Pearl Barnett, combined with other airlines to become American Airlines. Meacham Field today is a busy municipal airport.

215 Northeast 14th Street
NORTH FORT WORTH HIGH SCHOOL AND M. G. ELLIS ELEMENTARY SCHOOL

This two-story red brick building cost $35,000 when it was opened in 1906. Known as the North Side Public School, it served both elementary and high school students. Listed in the National Register of Historic Places.

Samuels Avenue
TRADERS' OAK

Henry Clay Daggett and Archibald Leonard established a trading post on this site in 1849. In 1850, the first county election was held under this tree, and Birdville was voted the county seat. Historical Marker placed by the Tarrant County Historical Society.

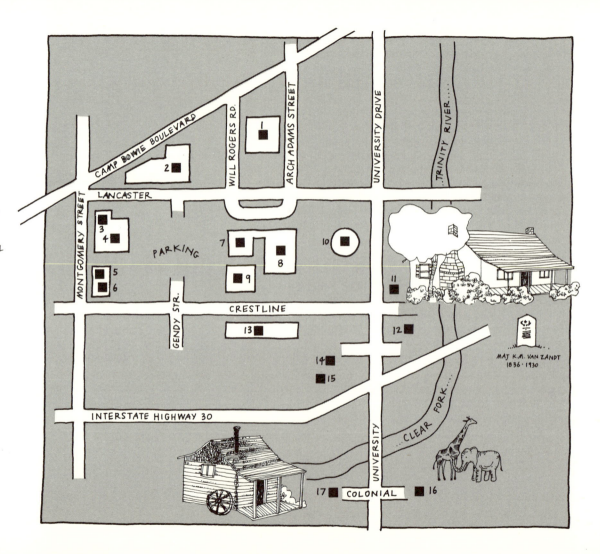

6.

The Cultural District

For a city its size, Forth Worth boasts an unusually fine museum complex and cultural district. This sprawling area on the city's near West Side includes museums, an auditorium-coliseum-exhibition hall complex, and the city's nearby botanical garden. The district was formerly known as Amon Carter Square in honor of Amon G. Carter, Fort Worth's outstanding civic leader of the twentieth century.

Born in a log cabin in North Central Texas, Carter came to Fort Worth in 1905 as advertising manager for *The Fort Worth Star*. In 1923, he bought control of the newspaper which by then had absorbed its rival, *The Telegram*. During the years he directed the *Fort Worth Star-Telegram*, Carter led the business community, bringing new business and industry to the county. He was responsible for locating several major oil companies in Fort Worth, along with a U.S. Public Health Hospital and the Consolidated-Vultee Aircraft Corporation, forerunner of today's General Dynamics. He was a leader in the construction of the Hotel Texas, The Fort Worth Club, Harris Methodist Hospital, and Amon Carter YMCA Camp. A confidante of politicians and friend of such notable figures as Franklin Delano Roosevelt and Will Rogers, Carter was in large part responsible for bringing the aviation industry to Fort Worth.

The many public buildings and facilities in Fort Worth which bear the Carter name testify to the wide range of his interests and accomplishments on behalf of Fort Worth and West Texas. The Carter family remains active in civic affairs today.

3501 Camp Bowie Boulevard
AMON CARTER MUSEUM

Established in 1961 through the will of the late Amon G. Carter, Sr., the museum houses an outstanding collection of American art. It began with Carter's personal collection of paintings and sculpture by Frederic Remington and Charles M. Russell and has been expanded to include works of other Western artists such as Thomas Moran,

Albert Bierstadt, and Alfred Jacob Miller as well as an excellent selection of nineteenth and early-twentieth century American art by William Michael Harnett, John Frederick Peto, Martin Johnson Heade, William Merritt Chase, and Stuart Davis, among others. The museum also exhibits selections from a large and impressive collection of prints and photographs, and maintains a schedule of changing exhibitions.

The building, designed by architect Philip Johnson of New York City, is constructed of Texas shellstone, the interior of bronze and teak. The English artist Henry Moore's *Upright Motives 1, 2, and 7* dominate the east end of the plaza. A small reference library, specializing in American art and history, is available by appointment during regular business hours.

West Lancaster and University Drive
CASA MAÑANA

In 1936, the Texas State Centennial was celebrated in Dallas. To attract its share of tourists, Fort Worth conceived of a Frontier Celebration and brought in Billy Rose, Broadway's top producer, to direct it. Rose designed Casa Mañana (literally, House of Tomorrow), a cabaret show on the world's largest revolving stage, as the main attraction. President Franklin D. Roosevelt opened the first show by remote control from a fishing boat off the coast of Maine. Among the featured entertainers for the centennial year was Sally Rand of the famous fan dance.

Casa Mañana ran for two years after the centennial and attracted national attention, bringing stars from California and New York. Wayne King, Eddie Cantor, Martha Ray, Ray Bolger, Charlie McCarthy and Edgar Bergen all performed on the outdoor stage. The theater was eventually razed because it was too expensive to produce the large-scale shows required by the big stage.

In the late 1950s, Casa Mañana was revived in a new building just east of the site of the old revolving stage. A geodesic-domed theater seating about 1800 persons made Casa the first permanent theater in the round under a roof. At that time, most summer musicals played in outdoor tents, but developers thought a tent impractical in the Texas heat. The dome construction made air conditioning economically feasible. Owned by the City of Fort Worth, the theater is leased to Casa Mañana, a non-profit educational and cultural organization.

The large gold and white theater organ in Casa Mañana was saved by the F. Howard Walsh family when the old Worth Theater was razed in 1972. Completely restored, the six-ton instrument has a xylophone, glockenspiel, marimba, vibraharp, cathedral chime, bass drum, and tom-tom.

Southeast corner of University Drive and Lancaster
FARRINGTON FIELD

Opened September, 1939, this field seats 19,450 people and is named in honor of the former Director of Physical Education in the Fort Worth Schools. It is used principally for athletic events presented by the Fort Worth Independent School District and is owned by the district. A concrete bas-relief on the stadium's west side was created by Fort Worth sculptor Evaline Sellors.

1309 Montgomery
FORT WORTH ART MUSEUM

The Fort Worth Art Museum grew out of the public library and the activities of the Fort Worth Art League. The present building was constructed in 1954 and remodeled in 1974. While the changing exhibitions emphasize modern and contemporary art, the permanent collection includes outstanding paintings by Thomas Eakins, George Inness, and others. The contemporary collection includes significant works by Pablo Picasso, Robert Rauschenberg, Andy Warhol, and many others.

The museum also presents frequent lectures, films, and performances.

Adjacent to the museum is William Edrington Scott Theater, one of the finest intimate theaters in the country today and home of the Fort Worth Theatre. It seats 500 people and was built with funds from the will of William Edrington Scott, which provided for continued cultural advancement of Fort Worth. The annual Christmas production of *The Littlest Wiseman*, presented here, is a highpoint of the holiday season in Fort Worth.

University Drive north of I-30
FORT WORTH BOTANICAL GARDEN

This municipal garden, built on an old gravel pit, features walks, pools, shelter houses, year-round horticultural displays, a scented garden for the blind and a six-acre Japanese garden with lagoons. Covering seventy seven acres, the garden has 14,000 rose bushes, more than 2,000 different plants and 150 varieties of trees.

1101 Will Rogers Road West
KIMBELL ART MUSEUM

Opened in 1972, the Kimbell Art Museum has achieved international renown through its outstanding art collection, the innovative building designed by the late Louis I. Kahn, and its series of spectacular, international exhibitions.

The permanent collection includes works by such well-known masters as Rembrandt, Gainsborough, Reynolds, Rubens, Goya, Pissarro, Monet, de la Tour, and El Greco. Selections of Asian, African, and pre-Columbian works are also on display.

The building is a series of self-supporting cycloidal vaults of post-tensioned concrete, based on a commitment to the use of natural light. This enables the visitor to see each work of art in the same changing conditions of light in which the artist created it. It received the Honor Award of the American Institute of Architects in 1975, the highest award for architectural excellence in the nation.

Exhibitions change frequently and include popular and well-known works from all over the world. In addition, the museum presents lectures, symposia, films, and other programs on a regular basis.

1501 Montgomery
MUSEUM OF SCIENCE AND HISTORY

This museum contains the Noble Planetarium, one of the top ten in the country, along with The Hall of Man and His Possessions, The Hall of Texas History, The May

Owen Hall of Medical Sciences, and exhibits on anthropology, archeology, history, geology, natural science and wildlife. There is also an exhibit of the personal effects of General William Jenkins Worth. Various rotating exhibits and more than 250 educational classes are scheduled throughout the year.

The multi-million dollar Omni Theater encircles an audience by filmed projections on an eighty-foot curved screen and features films on such topics as space exploration and the Great Barrier Reef.

3300 West Lancaster
WILL ROGERS MEMORIAL COLISEUM AND AUDITORIUM

This municipal complex, site of the annual Southwestern Exposition and Fat Stock Show, is named after Will Rogers, a close friend of Amon G. Carter. Carter was in Washington, D.C., when Rogers was killed in an airplane crash in Alaska. He immediately returned here, flew to California and from there to Alaska to accompany Rogers' body back to California. Because Rogers had frequently called Fort Worth his second home, Carter saw that the auditorium and coliseum were named for the famed humorist and commissioned sculptor Electra Waggoner to create the bronze of Rogers riding his favorite pony, Soapsuds, which stands in front of the complex. The statue is called *Riding into the Sunset*.

Built in the 1930s as a WPA project and first used for the Southwestern Exposition and Fat Stock Show in the 1940s, the complex has been continuously enlarged and modernized. Today it is used for a variety of public activities in addition to the annual stock show.

The dome of the coliseum features a unique design of radial arches. It and the complex tower were designed by Herbert M. Hinckley, and a Texas Historical Marker, honoring Hinckley, was placed in 1971.

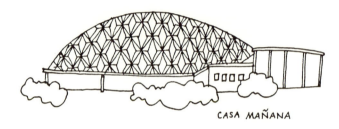
CASA MAÑANA

7.

Fort Worth—West Side

Veterans' Park, 4100 Camp Bowie Boulevard
CAMP BOWIE

 HEADQUARTERS of the 36th Division, United States Army, from 1917 to 1919, Camp Bowie was established to train National Guard units from Texas and Oklahoma for service in World War I. It was named for James Bowie of Alamo fame.

 When the first units arrived at the camp, it was open prairie, still used for grazing, and soldiers slept in knee-deep Johnson grass. Some 25,000 men were shipped to France from the camp in July, 1918. They captured St. Etienne-a-Arnes and participated in the Meuse-Argonne campaign which resulted in the defeat and eventual surrender of the German army. The 36th Division was demobilized during the summer of 1919, and the camp reverted to civilian use by August, 1920.

 The major roadway through the camp, now called Camp Bowie Boulevard, was originally known as Arlington Heights Boulevard, denoting the name of this city addition which was first developed in the late nineteenth century by the American Land and Investment Company. Ye Arlington Inn at Merrick and Byers dispensed hospitality; streetcar lines connected the area to the downtown district; and a dam created Lake Como to furnish power and water for houses in the new area. Financial depression broke the investment company in 1890, Ye Arlington Inn burned, and the streetcar system was abandoned. Development of Camp Bowie during World War I brought new growth to the area, however, and it is today one of the city's fine inner-city residential areas.

 Camp Bowie Boulevard, originally simply narrow strips of asphalt paving flanking streetcar tracks, was paved with durable Thurber bricks in the late 1920s. The suggestion of repaving the road and covering the bricks was abandoned in the 1980s after heated protest from citizens. A Texas Historical Marker, placed in 1978, describes the historic importance of Camp Bowie Boulevard. An earlier marker, placed in 1973, gives the history of Camp Bowie.

In 1932, elm trees were planted in the park to commemorate George Washington's bicentennial, and in 1973, the Daughters of the American Revolution planted trees to commemorate soldiers missing in action or detained as prisoners of war.

Carswell Avenue Road, off Highway 10 near intersection with Roaring Springs Road
CARSWELL AIR FORCE BASE

Carswell Air Force Base was established in conjunction with the Consolidated Vultee Aircraft Plant, which was built here in 1941 when the government established a bomber plant. At the groundbreaking, an exuberant Major General told the audience, "We're starting to dig Hitler's grave this afternoon." During World War II, the plant built the B-24 bomber and the Convair B-32 and employed at its peak 35,000 people, making it the largest industry in the city. Today, the multimillion dollar international plant is known as the Convair Division of General Dynamics and is one of the largest if not the largest industry in Tarrant County.

Tarrant Field, built by the army adjacent to the aircraft plant, was renamed in honor of Major Horace S. Carswell, a Fort Worth native and holder of a Congressional medal of Honor who was killed in China during World War II. At the time of the name change in 1948, the base had been taken over by the Air Force and it remains an active Air Force base today.

2900 Crestline
DRAG STONE

The drag stone in the yard of the Van Zandt log house was dug from the courthouse bluff by Louis Wetmore, a native of Rodenburg who left Germany to escape military duty but arrived in the United States in time to fight in the Mexican War (1846–1848) with Major Ripley Arnold. Wetmore was with Major Arnold when Fort Worth was founded and remained here after being mustered out. Killed in the Civil War, he is remembered by the drag stone he pulled by oxen, from 1853–1861, to smooth rutted roads and knock down high grass so surveyors could mark boundaries. Marker, 1924, by the Daughters of the American Revolution.

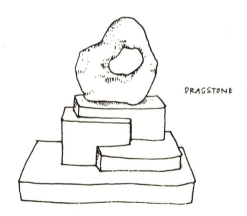
DRAGSTONE

6350 West Freeway, Southern Baptist Radio-Television Commission
LAST SUPPER TABLEAU

This tableau is a wax interpretation of the fresco by Leonard da Vinci on the wall of the upper room of Santa Maria alle Grazie church in Milan. Commissioned by William Fleming, father of Mrs. F. Howard Walsh, the tableau was completed through an endowment created by the F. Howard Walsh foundation. It was done by a family who had been making lifelike wax figures for generations. Tapes are provided in English, Spanish and Portugese, and the tableau is open to the public during business hours.

Turnaround at Greenwood Cemetery Main Entrance, White Settlement Road
TURNER OAK

Charles Turner, one of the first settlers in Tarrant County and a captain in the Texas Rangers, buried gold under this tree and later used it to provide financial aid for Fort Worth during the critical years of the Reconstruction period. The Texas Forest Service estimates that this oak is over 700 years old.

Historical Marker placed in 1954 by the Daughters of the American Revolution.

6100 Western Place (I-30 at the Guilford exit)
THE WESTERN COMPANY MUSEUM

Museum displays show the geology of hydrocarbons as well as the history of the petroleum industry and of The Western Company. Chemistry, physics and astronomy are used to demonstrate the application of science in the development of new technologies. Intricate scientific processes, both natural and man-made, are explained to museum visitors through demonstrations, exhibitions and written presentations. Open to the public.

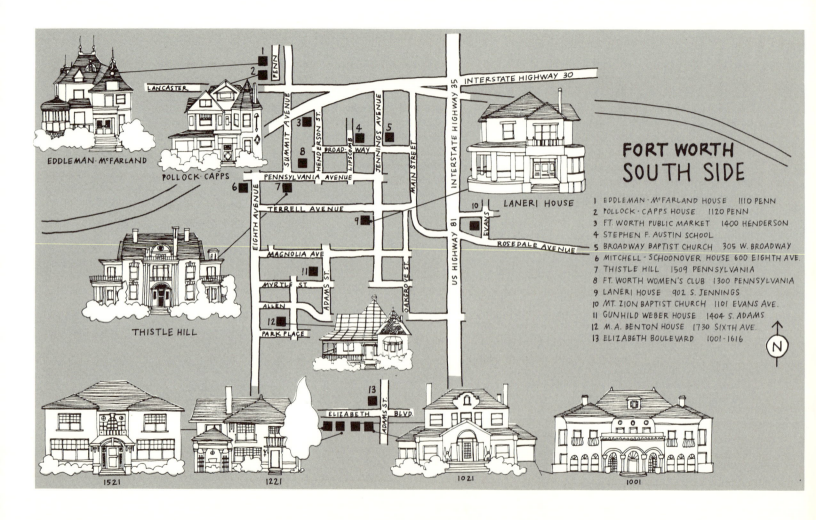

8.

Fort Worth—South Side

2300 Hemphill
EDNA GLADNEY HOME

In 1887, the Reverend Isaac Z. T. Morris and his wife began taking orphans and abandoned children into their home for care. Their work led to the 1904 chartering of the Texas Children's Home and Aid Society. The society's primary mission was to place children in well-chosen adoptive homes.

In 1910, Mrs. Edna Gladney became director of the home. A crusader on behalf of children and unwed mothers, Mrs. Gladney was named superintendent in 1927. Her work resulted in permanent housing for the society, expanded services, and legislative and social reforms. Her accomplishments received wide public notice, and her story was dramatized in the 1941 movie, *Blossoms In The Dust*. The society and its facilities were renamed The Edna Gladney Home in 1950.

Today, the home has a five-acre campus with dormitories and apartments, educational facilities, and its own accredited hospital. Its programs include New Hope, an adoptive service for children with special needs, and career development programs for unwed mothers. It provides care for about 600 girls annually and places about 400 children in adoptive homes. The National Committee For Adoption has called it the outstanding maternity home in the nation.

Texas Historical Marker, 1974.

Between Eighth Avenue and College Avenue
ELIZABETH BOULEVARD HISTORICAL DISTRICT

Elizabeth Boulevard is the central street in the Ryan Place Addition, a neighborhood of grand homes developed by John C. Ryan, who foresaw the need for an affluent neighborhood close to the business district. The area was home to cattlemen and oilmen, and Elizabeth Boulevard came to be called "Silver Slipper Row."

In 1917, C. P. "Daredevil Cal" Rodgers landed his

1001 ELIZ BLVD   1021 ELIZ BLVD   1080 ELIZ BLVD

plane in a pasture in the Ryan Place Addition on his pioneer transcontinental flight.

The elaborate entry gates and the first house, the W. T. Fry home at 1112 Elizabeth, were built in 1911. Ryan's own home is located at 1302 Elizabeth Boulevard and was built in 1915.

Construction of elaborate mansions and homes in this area continued until the Depression. After that time, smaller bungalows were built amongst the large homes.

Texas Historical Marker, 1981; Elizabeth Boulevard is listed in the National Register of Historic Places. Many houses on the boulevard also have individual markers.

University Drive and Colonial Parkway
FOREST PARK ZOO

The oldest continuous zoo site in Texas, the Forest Park Zoo was established in 1909 when three park commissioners bought a group of animals from a traveling carnival. The zoo had only temporary pens and shelters until 1923, when a stone shelter was built for an elephant named Queen Tut. Outstanding features in the zoo today include the James R. Record Aquarium; the herpetarium which houses one of the finest and most diverse collections of reptiles and amphibians in any zoo; an African diorama which displays zebra, springbok, ostrich, gazelle, stork, vultures, cheetahs, lions and other African animals live in their natural habitat; the Primate House with concrete "ape-proof" trees, swinging ropes, a redwood bridge and pools with showers which the apes can activate; a walk-through aviary; and an infant care facility for small mammals and birds. The zoo also has an extensive education department and presents slides and movies on a sixty-foot wrap-around screen. Formal programs include live animal presentations, guided tours with docents, and summer classes. Texas Historical Marker, 1984.

University Drive and Colonial Parkway
LOG CABIN VILLAGE

These log cabins are authentic, built in the last century by pioneer families and moved to this village in 1966 from a variety of locations in Texas. They are made of oak, cedar and pine logs, prepared for construction with such tools as the axe, broadaxe and adze. Each cabin is furnished with authentic furniture and clothing which would have been found in a typical cabin at that time. The dog-trot cabin of Isaac Parker in the village was one of the last homes of Cynthia Ann Parker after she was recaptured from the Comanches in 1860. Spinning, quilting and candle-making are demonstrated in various cabins, and the village includes a working mill where corn is ground and cornmeal offered for sale.

3600 Wichita Street
MASONIC HOME AND SCHOOL OF TEXAS

In July 1898, Fort Worth Masonic Lodge #148, offered 200 acres to the Grand Lodge of Texas to support its interest in educating orphans of Masons. The land was accepted for a home and school, and additional acreage was purchased to provide access to public roads. The home opened in October 1899. It has an independent school district with all grades through high school.

General Services Administration
5051 James Avenue
OLD 610 LOCOMOTIVE

Old 610, a Lima Superpower Steam engine built for the Texas and Pacific in 1927, was completely restored for the Bicentennial. It pulled the American Freedom Train across Texas and was later used as an excursion locomotive. It is owned by the 610 Historical Association which raised money for its restoration, and is listed on the National Register of Historic Sites. The locomotive sits on land adjacent to the National Archives and Records Service of the General Services Administration, which holds extensive government records.

Seminary & I-35
SEMINARY SOUTH

Fort Worth's first major suburban shopping center, opened in 1962, is located on the site of Katy Lake, a man-made watering place for cattle drives and a source of water for the steam engines of the Katy Railroad. The lake was drained by Sears-Roebuck Company after the land was purchased from private owners.

2000 West Seminary Drive
SOUTHWESTERN THEOLOGICAL SEMINARY

Chartered in 1908 for graduate education in Christian ministries, the seminary was moved here from Waco in 1910. The original 200-acre campus tract and the first building, Fort Worth Hall, were gifts from the people of

South Side

Fort Worth. Although the campus shrank in size when land was sold during the Depression, land acquisitions in recent years have returned it to the orginal 200-acre size. The grounds, noted for their blooming flower beds, are maintained as an avocation by a retired horticulturist. Of special interest is the A. Webb Roberts Library, which includes among its collections the Charles D. Tandy Archaeological Museum, open to the public.

Today, with 5000 students, Southwestern Theological Seminary is the largest graduate school of its kind in the world, with one of the largest doctoral programs in existence. It is under the control of the Southern Baptist Convention.

Texas Historical Marker, 1972.

2800 South University Drive
TEXAS CHRISTIAN UNIVERSITY

In 1869, a group of Fort Worth citizens invited Addison and Randolph Clark to set up a private school. The young preacher-teacher brothers taught classes in the Masonic lodge in what was then a cattle town. They planned a permanent academy and bought land for it, but during that boomtown period the disreputable area known as Hell's Half Acre developed next to their building site. The brothers chose an alternative site forty miles away in Thorp Spring. The Add-Ran Male and Female College opened its doors there in 1873, but the isolation of this site proved a hindrance and the school, by now affiliated with the Christian Church of Texas, moved to Waco in 1895.

In 1902, the school's name was changed to Texas Christian University. A fire destroyed the main building in 1910, and the trustees accepted an offer to move to Fort Worth. Classes were held in rented downtown buildings for a year, then moved to the current campus about three miles southwest of downtown.

About 6800 students enroll annually at TCU. Half of them live in sixteen residence halls on campus. Another forty-five buildings house programs in more than fifty fields of study. TCU is one of the few church-related universities to host a Phi Beta Kappa chapter and to grant the Ph.D. degree.

Two galleries, the Moudy Building Exhibition Space and the Brown-Lupton Student Center Gallery, are open to the public. They feature traveling exhibitions as well as exhibits by faculty, students and invited artists.

Eleventh Avenue and Cooper Street
TRADER'S OAK

An old metal sign on this large live oak tree, on the southwest corner of the intersection, reads "Historic Tree First Indian Trading Post 1843 Established by First Settlers, Capt. Terrell and John R. Lusk." The date and origin of the sign are unknown, and the information cannot be verified.

1302–26 Pennsylvania Avenue
THE WOMAN'S CLUB OF FORT WORTH

The Woman's Club of Fort Worth was founded in 1923 in a house donated by Mrs. Etta O. Newby. Miss Anna Shelton was the first president. Today, the club owns several buildings of historical interest, each with its own historical marker and each named for a prominent club member. *Florence Shuman Hall* at 1302 Pennsylvania, is a cottage built in 1905 and rebuilt in 1910 by civic leader W. R. Edrington. *Ida Saunders Hall*, at 1316 Pennsylvania, is the former home of William Edrington Scott, built in 1903. *Margaret Meacham Hall* was built in 1905 and sold in 1920 to the Baptist Hospital as a nurses' residence. *The William G. Newby Memorial Building*, 1316 Pennsylvania, was built about 1912 by Heinrich Frerichs, a buyer for large German cotton interests who was later revealed as a high ranking espionage officer for Germany. The building was then occupied by the U.S. Military. Mrs. William G. Newby bought it in 1923 and gave it to the club as a memorial to her husband. *The Junior Woman's Building* at Ballinger and Pennsylvania, the former W. M. Moore home, completes the block of women's buildings. Texas Historical Marker, 1976.

1221 ELIZ BLVD

1508 ELIZ BLVD

1521 ELIZ BLVD

South Side

9.

Fort Worth—East Side

Intersection of Highways 360 and 183
AMON CARTER FIELD

 Known as Greater Southwest International Airport, this airport was built in the late 1940s. Its plans evoked a spectacular battle with Dallas civic leaders who objected to the location of the airport and took the battle all the way to the U. S. Congress. It was built with federal funds. Fort Worth planners were stymied in their plan to name the airport for Amon G. Carter by a government rule which forbad the naming of an international airport after a living individual. However, they could and did name the administration building and the airfield after Carter in recognition of his accomplishments in bringing aviation to Fort Worth. (Please see separate entry, The Cultural District, for biographical data on this civic leader.)

 It was due to Carter's efforts that the first planes flew from Fort Worth. In 1911, when the International Aviators—three Frenchmen and a Swiss citizen—toured the nation, Carter raised $5000 to bring them to Fort Worth. In spite of dangerously high winds, the four put on an exhibition before a crowd of 15,000 gathered in the old Driving Park between White Settlement Road and West Seventh Street.

 Later, Carter worked tirelessly for the establishment of a municipal airport (please see entry for Meacham Field, Fort Worth–North Side) and the building of an aircraft plant here (please see entry for Carswell Air Force Base, Fort Worth–West Side).

 Amon Carter Field never reached its full potential because airlines objected to landing twice so close together, once at this field and then again in Dallas. The FAA and Civil Aeronautics Board decided federal money should be channeled to an airport that would serve both Dallas and Fort Worth. The Dallas/Fort Worth International Airport was built almost directly adjacent to this field. The main north-south runway is now Amon Carter Boulevard in a high quality business park.

1302–26 Pennsylvania Avenue
THE WOMAN'S CLUB OF FORT WORTH

The Woman's Club of Fort Worth was founded in 1923 in a house donated by Mrs. Etta O. Newby. Miss Anna Shelton was the first president. Today, the club owns several buildings of historical interest, each with its own historical marker and each named for a prominent club member. *Florence Shuman Hall* at 1302 Pennsylvania, is a cottage built in 1905 and rebuilt in 1910 by civic leader W. R. Edrington. *Ida Saunders Hall*, at 1316 Pennsylvania, is the former home of William Edrington Scott, built in 1903. *Margaret Meacham Hall* was built in 1905 and sold in 1920 to the Baptist Hospital as a nurses' residence. *The William G. Newby Memorial Building*, 1316 Pennsylvania, was built about 1912 by Heinrich Frerichs, a buyer for large German cotton interests who was later revealed as a high ranking espionage officer for Germany. The building was then occupied by the U.S. Military. Mrs. William G. Newby bought it in 1923 and gave it to the club as a memorial to her husband. *The Junior Woman's Building* at Ballinger and Pennsylvania, the former W. M. Moore home, completes the block of women's buildings. Texas Historical Marker, 1976.

1221 ELIZ BLVD

1508 ELIZ BLVD

1521 ELIZ BLVD

South Side

9.

Fort Worth—East Side

Intersection of Highways 360 and 183
AMON CARTER FIELD

KNOWN AS Greater Southwest International Airport, this airport was built in the late 1940s. Its plans evoked a spectacular battle with Dallas civic leaders who objected to the location of the airport and took the battle all the way to the U. S. Congress. It was built with federal funds. Fort Worth planners were stymied in their plan to name the airport for Amon G. Carter by a government rule which forbad the naming of an international airport after a living individual. However, they could and did name the administration building and the airfield after Carter in recognition of his accomplishments in bringing aviation to Fort Worth. (Please see separate entry, The Cultural District, for biographical data on this civic leader.)

It was due to Carter's efforts that the first planes flew from Fort Worth. In 1911, when the International Aviators—three Frenchmen and a Swiss citizen—toured the nation, Carter raised $5000 to bring them to Fort Worth. In spite of dangerously high winds, the four put on an exhibition before a crowd of 15,000 gathered in the old Driving Park between White Settlement Road and West Seventh Street.

Later, Carter worked tirelessly for the establishment of a municipal airport (please see entry for Meacham Field, Fort Worth–North Side) and the building of an aircraft plant here (please see entry for Carswell Air Force Base, Fort Worth–West Side).

Amon Carter Field never reached its full potential because airlines objected to landing twice so close together, once at this field and then again in Dallas. The FAA and Civil Aeronautics Board decided federal money should be channeled to an airport that would serve both Dallas and Fort Worth. The Dallas/Fort Worth International Airport was built almost directly adjacent to this field. The main north-south runway is now Amon Carter Boulevard in a high quality business park.

Related Sites
AVIATION INDUSTRY

    Barron Field, Fort Worth—South Side
    Carswell Air Force Base, Fort Worth—West Side
    D/FW International Airport—Euless
    Elizabeth Boulevard, Fort Worth—South Side
    Hicks Field, Unincorporated Areas
    Meacham Field, Fort Worth—North Side

Spur 303 (East Rosedale)
at the end of Handley Drive
HANDLEY POWER PLANT
AND LAKE ERIE

This power plant was built by the Northern Texas Traction Company to generate electrical power for the Fort Worth-to-Dallas Interurban (please see the following entry). Lake Erie, which supplied water as a cooling source for the plant, was converted into a park with a two-story auditorium extending over the edge of the lake. When interurban traffic declined in the 1930s, the park was closed. With increased electrical demands, the Handley plant was expanded and Lake Erie became part of Lake Arlington, the new water source, in 1957. Engineers had projected it would take three to four years to fill the new lake, but bountiful rainfall filled it in only twenty-seven days.
Texas Historical Marker, 1980.

Electric Service Company Power Station
HANDLEY STATION, FORT WORTH-DALLAS
INTERURBAN

In 1901 the Texas Legislature authorized the Northern Texas Traction Company of Fort Worth to extend rail service to Dallas. The interurban system, powered by overhead electrical lines, was completed one year later. The Crimson Limited Express reached speeds of ninety miles per hour. On regular runs, passengers could flag the train and board at any point, so delays were frequent. When paved roads were constructed between the two cities in the 1930s, rail traffic declined. The last train made the interurban run on Christmas Eve, 1934.

The Texas Electric Service Company gate is the approximate location of the Handley Depot for the interurban line. Directly north, between the present railroad tracks and Lancaster Avenue, was the Handley Depot of the Texas and Pacific Railroad.
Texas Historical Marker, 1980.

Precinct Line Road and Randol Mill Road
RANDOL MILL

In 1856, Archibald F. Leonard built a dam and grain mill at this site. Since farmers occasionally had to wait several days for grain to be processed, the mill became a community gathering place. Leonard's Mill was burned in widespread abolition violence on July 8, 1860. Reopened by 1862, it served Tarrant and surrounding counties during the Civil War. The mill, a circular saw, and a cotton gin were all powered by a water-driven turbine. R. A. (Bob) Randol purchased the mill in 1876 and operated it until his death in 1922.

Only sections of stonework along the river bank remain of the original mill. These are found about one hundred yards west of the Precinct Line Road bridge.

Texas Historical Marker, 1979.

3101 East Rosedale
TEXAS WESLEYAN COLLEGE

Texas Wesleyan College was founded in 1891 by the Methodist Episcopal Church, South, and was named Polytechnic College, meaning literally "many arts and sciences." The surrounding neighborhood, known as Poly, takes its name from the institution. Built on land donated by three men from an early Fort Worth family, the college was later called Texas Woman's College and then Texas Wesleyan College.

Wesleyan is located on more than seventy-four acres on one of the highest points in the city. Among its historic Buildings are Oneal-Sells Hall, now the college administration building. It was built of Texas limestone in 1902, modernized in 1963, and extensively remodeled in 1980. A Texas Historical Marker was placed on it in 1966. Ann Waggoner Hall, constructed in 1891, enlarged in 1905 and renovated in 1968, houses faculty offices and the John G. Anderson Chapel. The oldest college structure continuously in use in Tarrant County, the building was a gift from Dan Waggoner, a noted Texas rancher, in honor of his wife. Ann Waggoner Hall received a Texas Historical Marker in 1967. Also of interest is the Alumni Center across Rosedale Street from the main campus. It was formerly the home of S. S. Dillow, a pioneer in the Polytechnic neighborhood who opened the area's first business, a grocery store. The two-story home was built in 1912 and willed to the college by the last surviving member of the Dillow family in 1981.

3900 Barnett Street
WBAP RADIO

Founded by civic leader Amon G. Carter, WBAP radio was one of America's first radio stations when it went on the air in 1922. A powerful 50,000-watt station, it can be heard from coast to coast. An exhibit in the reception area displays technological equipment used in the early days of radio. WBAP-TV, now KXAS-TV, also founded by Carter, aired its first program in 1948, featuring a public appearance by President Harry Truman. WBAP-TV made the first color telecast in Texas in 1954.

Texas Historical Subject Marker, 1967.

10.
Suburban Communities & Unincorporated Areas

Arlington

2225 East Randol Mill Road
ARLINGTON DOWNS RACE TRACK

Because of his stable of fine thoroughbreds and quarter horses, Texas rancher and oilman W. T. Waggoner built Arlington Downs, a one-and-a-quarter-mile racetrack with a 6,000-seat grandstand. Waggoner and his sons, Guy and Paul, campaigned for parimutuel betting, and it was legalized in Texas from 1934 to 1937. Used for rodeos and other events, the racetrack and its buildings were razed in 1958.
Texas Historical Marker, 1978.

Lake Arlington Golf Course, 7th tee
Lakewood Drive and Highway 303 (Pioneer Parkway)
BATTLE OF VILLAGE CREEK

In the 1830s, this Trinity River tributary served as a sanctuary for several Indian tribes who made frequent raids on frontier settlements. In 1841, major attacks were reported in Fannin and Red River counties. Edward H. Tarrant, Brigadier General of the Republic of Texas Militia, led a company of seventy volunteers on an expedition against Indian villages in this area. Reportedly, twelve Indians and one soldier were killed. As a result of this battle, Indian tribes began moving west. Those who remained in the area were later removed under the terms of the 1843 treaty signed at Bird's Fort (please see entry under The Founding of Tarrant County and Camp Worth). Much of the battle site is now under water.

Archeological excavations along this tributary have unearthed evidence of inhabitation by food gatherers and hunters for nearly 9000 years. A Historical Marker placed in 1936 is located on Highway 303; a Texas Historical Marker was placed at the site in 1980.

Arkansas Lane and Matlock Road, Founder's Park
MARROW BONE SPRING

President of the Texas Republic, Sam Houston, visited this site in 1843, and in 1845 a trading post was licensed to open near this spring. In 1851, Johnson's Station, the first post office in Tarrant County, opened at this site. Johnson sold his rights to land surrounding the spring in 1852, but the village of Johnson's Station flourished for many years. Texas Historical Marker, 1979; listed as a National Archeological Site.

621 West Arkansas Lane
SCHOOL, ARLINGTON'S OLDEST

This board and batten structure was built in 1909, following a fire which burned the North Side School at 433 North Center. Two grades met in this building for one term until a new brick school was built. Contractor Joseph Crawley, who built this schoolhouse, then bought this building and moved it to 304 South Pecan where it served as his office. It was moved to this site adjacent to the Middleton Tate Johnson Plantation Cemetery in 1977. Texas Historical Marker, for the cemetery, placed in 1979. Please see separate entries for Jopling-Melear Cabin, P. A. Watson log house (Arlington), and Middleton Tate Johnson Cemetery (Arlington).

Highways I-30 and 360
SIX FLAGS OVER TEXAS

The six flags—Spanish, French, Mexican, Republic of Texas, Confederate and U.S.—which have flown over Texas are commemorated in the name of this amusement park, one of the earliest theme parks in the country. Replicas of historic places are on the grounds, and the exhibits vividly re-create the colorful history of the Lone Star State. Texas Historical Marker, 1966. In addition, the following attractions have individual markers:

Narrow Gauge Railway, with two engines built in 1887 and 1903 and rebuilt according to original specifications. The line symbolizes the many narrow gauge railroads which ran in Texas between 1853 and 1900. One line, the Great Sweetgum, Yabadam and Hoo Hoo was called the T.M.&C. (two mules and a car).

Replica of Fort Saint Louis, a fort established in 1685 on Matagorda Bay by the French explorer LaSalle and abandoned before 1689 because of Indian attacks.

Boom Town, a replica of the derricks that drilled the early deep oil wells in Texas, with the same rigging and tools used in 1920 to drill the Crowley No. 1, one of the deepest wells at that time.

Antique Hand Carved Carousel, typical of a popular entertainment in early Texas. The arrival of a traveling carnival with a horse-drawn carousel and a calliope was a great event in many communities.

Suburban Areas

800 South Cooper
THE UNIVERSITY OF TEXAS AT ARLINGTON

In 1894, L. M. Hammond and W. M. Trimble, M.D., Arlington city trustees, promised to found a college if they were winners in an upcoming election. Having won the election, they each donated $500 and pledged to sell fifteen five-year scholarships at $100 each. Land was donated by the Ditto and Collins Land Company, and a two-story frame building was put up. Tuition collected during the 1895–6 school year ranged from $1.50 to $3.50 per month, depending on the student's grade level. First called Arlington College, the school later became the Carlisle Military Academy, the Arlington Training School, Grubbs Vocational College, and Arlington State College. In 1917, when citizens donated 100 acres of land, the legislature voted to fund the college as a vocational school and put it under the direction of Texas A & M College. Since 1966, it has been part of the state university system, officially called The University of Texas at Arlington.

The University Art Gallery, located in the Fine Arts Building, has exhibits ranging from traveling shows of the work of nationally known artists to student exhibitions. Special Collections on the sixth floor of the library houses a rare collection of materials relating to the Texas War of Independence, an outstanding cartography library, and the Robertson's Collection of papers relating to Robertson's Colony, one of the first settlements in Texas. Both areas are open to the public.

The Berachah Home and Cemetery are located within the campus, in Doug Russell Park, just west of Cooper Street. The Berachah Rescue Society was organized in 1894 for the protection of homeless girls and unwed mothers. Ten buildings were located here, including a handkerchief factory and a print shop for publication of the *Purity Journal*. The cemetery was first used in 1904 for the burial of one of the residents. The home closed in 1935 but was used as an orphanage until 1942. Texas Historical Marker, 1980.

Azle

301 Church Street
AZLE SCHOOLS

Pioneer settler J. G. Reynolds probably started the first area school in the 1850s. Early classes met in log cabins and in the Ash Creek Baptist Church and were interrupted by Indian attacks and the Civil War. The Azle school system grew through consolidation with such neighboring communities as Promised Land, Steele, Slover, Sabathany, Liberty, Briar, Bluff Springs, and a local college. Texas Historical Marker, 1982.

FM 730, Six miles north of SH 199
KIOWA RAID ON WALNUT CREEK

A band of about sixty Kiowa warriors, under chiefs Satank and Satanta, raided the home of William Hamleton on Walnut Creek in April, 1867. They killed Mrs. Hamleton, the former Sally Allman, widow of James Myres, and took Lavina Myres, her half-brother Gus Hamleton, and her half-sister Sally Hamleton. Lavina and Gus were later traded but Mary was raised as a member of the Kiowa tribe. Known as To-Gome, she had seven children and lived until 1924.

The site of the raid is now underwater in the Eagle Mountain Reservoir, north of Highway 199 and east of the marker. Texas Historical Marker, 1983, sponsored by the Azle State Bank.

124 West Main
POST OFFICE

Originally named O'Bar, the Azle Post Office opened in 1881 and was located in a store. In 1916, Postmaster Cora Lovell moved the operation to a frame building where it remained until 1953. During the thirty-eight year term of Postmistress Elsie Gipson Parker, the post office also housed a small public library and became a community gathering place. In 1971, Azle was ranked a first class postal station, and a larger building was erected. Texas Historical Marker, 1979, sponsored by the Azle Museum and the Azle Chamber of Commerce.

Bedford

1801 School Lane
BEDFORD SCHOOL

The first classes in Bedford met in a log building during the early 1860s. After the Civil War, classes were held in a frame building north of this site. When it burned in 1882, Milton Moore deeded land here for the construction of Bedford College. A second fire in 1893 again destroyed the building. Local citizens raised money for an elementary school at this site, and it was used until 1908 when a two-story brick schoolhouse was built. That building was occupied until 1969 and is now used for storage by the Bedford Gas Company. Texas Historical Subject Marker, 1980, sponsored by the First State Bank of Bedford.

4200 Block, Bedford Road
GLASSCO SCHOOL

About 1877, a school was established on property belonging to Confederate veteran Daniel Glassco. Classes were held in a log cabin until it burned in 1899. School trustee William Evatt then gave an acre of land for another schoolhouse, and a new school district was created. Texas Historical Marker, 1983.

Benbrook

812 Mercedes Street, Benbrook Cemetery
GRAVE OF JAMES M. BENBROOK

Benbrook, a native of Indiana, brought his family to this area in 1876. The settlement was then known as Miranda. A veteran of the Union Army, Benbrook became a prominent farmer and landowner here. In 1880, when rail lines were completed and a depot constructed, the community was renamed Benbrook in his honor by the Texas and Pacific Railroad Company. Texas Historical Grave Marker, 1982.

Memorial Oak Drive near Benbrook Dam
BUR OAK, LARGEST IN TEXAS

This tree officially measures 210 inches in circumference, eighty-one feet in height, with an eighty-eight foot crown spread. The tree is on federal land leased to the City of Fort Worth and maintained by the Fort Worth Park and Recreation Department.

Euless

Intersection Highways 360 and 183
D/FW INTERNATIONAL AIRPORT

When it was opened in January 1974, this was the largest commercial aviation facility in the world. Covering 17,500 acres, it is as big as the New York City borough of Manhattan. Located equidistant between Dallas and Fort Worth business districts, the airport is the result of cooperation between the two cities that was not achieved in the late 1940s during the planning stage for Amon Carter Field.

When ground was being dug for the airport, construction crews uncovered the giant skeleton of a plesisaurus or water-moving dinosaur which lived some seventy million years ago.

Everman

Oak Grove Park, Oak Grove Road (in Commercial Park)
BARRON FIELD

Originally called Taliaferro Field No. 2, this was one of three World War I Flight Training Centers established in the county by Canadian troops. Hicks Field (see entry under Unincorporated Areas) and Carruthers Field (now covered by Lake Benbrook) were the other two. Built in November 1917, it was first used to train Canadian troops. In April 1918, American forces assumed command and renamed the field in memory of Cadet Robert J. Barron. Covering over 600 acres and housing as many as 150 officers and 900 unlisted men, the field sent six air squadrons to France before the war ended in November 1918. Among instructors here was Captain Vernon Castle, of the famed Vernon and Irene Castle dancing team. Castle was killed when his plane stalled and crashed on this field.

Barron Field was closed in 1921. Only the munitions building remains. Texas Historical Marker placed in 1976 by the Everman Garden Club.

Grapevine

Grapevine Municipal Golf Course (near 13th green)
ASH TREE, LARGEST IN TEXAS

When last measured, this tree was seventy-eight feet in height, with a circumference of 145 inches and a crown of sixty-eight feet. It is estimated to be 250 years old.

523 Main Street
J. E. FOUST & SON FUNERAL DIRECTORS

In 1880, at age nineteen, John Foust moved to Grapevine and started a general merchandise store which stocked coffins. He gradually added other services connected with the funeral home business. A civic leader, Foust helped with the establishment of other area businesses. His son, John E. Foust II, managed the funeral home and mercantile business until the 1960s. Texas Historical Marker, 1981.

205 Main in Liberty Park
GRAPEVINE, CITY OF

This historic marker tells the history of the City of Grapevine. Founded by settlers from Missouri in 1845, the community was named for the wild mustang grapes which grew profusely in the area. A federal post office was established in 1858. Prior to the Civil War, area farmers raised cattle for sale to Fort Worth.

During the 1870s, the village became known as Dunnville. In the 1880s, it thrived as a shipping center for cotton, grain, truck crops and dairy products. In 1907, the town was incorporated, the name changed back to Grapevine. A dam built on Denton Creek formed Lake Grapevine in 1952. In 1974, the D/FW Regional Airport opened within the city limits. Texas Historical Marker, 1979.

332 Main
THE GRAPEVINE SUN

Benjamin R. Wall first published the *Grapevine Sun* in 1895 when he was nineteen. The paper was sold in 1897 to James E. Keeling, a native of England; Keeling's son took over as editor in 1912, publishing the paper with the help of his wife, Grady. In 1953, on William's death, his daughter, Zena Keeling Oxford, became publisher. *The Sun* was sold following her death in 1976, ending the family connection which had lasted eighty years and spanned three generations. Texas Historical Marker, 1980.

Haltom City

6108 Broadway Avenue
COURTHOUSE, TARRANT COUNTY'S FIRST

When Birdville was Tarrant County's first county seat (see entry under The Founding of Tarrant County and Camp Worth), eighty acres were set aside for public use, and a courthouse foundation built on the donated land. Texas Historical Marker, 1968.

Hurst

Precinct Line and Harwood
FLORENCE SCHOOL

In the 1890s, the forerunner of Florence School was called Green Glade. It was sold to pay for the one-room Florence Schoolhouse at this site in 1903. The new school offered grades one through eight and had an average enrollment of thirty pupils. The term ran from October, after cotton harvest, to May, the beginning of cotton chopping. The school building also served as a community center and a site for elections. Texas Historical Marker, 1979, sponsored by Jenkins Garrett, first Chairman of Tarrant County Junior College.

1505 Precinct Line Road
HURST, WILLIAM LETCHWORTH

This marker tells the story of the Confederate veteran for whom the community of Hurst is named. A native of Tennessee, Hurst saw action near Vicksburg, Mississippi. Following the surrender of his unit to General Ulysses S. Grant in 1863 and his subsequent release, he joined in the reorganization of his outfit as the Sixty-first Tennessee Mounted Infantry and was captured again near Tennessee, spending the last two years of the war in military prisons in Kentucky and Illinois.

In 1870, Hurst and his wife joined other residents of Claiborne County, Tennessee, in migrating to Texas where he became a prominent land speculator. In 1903, he granted a right-of-way across his farm for construction of the Rock Island rail line. In exchange, the company named a rail stop and depot for him.

The father of fourteen, Hurst had over 100 grandchildren. Many of his descendants are still active in community affairs, and in 1983, the mayor of Hurst was a descendant of his. Texas Historical Marker, 1981.

Keller

US 377, south of Keller
KELLER, COMMUNITY OF

In 1881, when the T & P Railroad came through this area, druggist H. W. Wood set aside forty acres for the village of Athol. Within a year, the name was changed to honor railroad construction crew foreman John C. Keller. A post office was established in 1886, and a Union Church building erected the same year. By that time, Keller boasted two hotels, three doctors, a newspaper, a school, and several agricultural businesses. The community was incorporated in 1958. Texas Historical Marker, 1980.

Mansfield

Business 287, one-half mile north of downtown Mansfield
EARLE C. DRISKELL MONUMENT

Driskell, a newspaperman, was among the first to recognize that the automobile was about to replace the horse and buggy. Courageous enough to put his ideas into writing, Driskell did much to influence the public to recognize the need for paved roads. A private marker was erected in 1938 after Commissioner Joe Thannisch discovered a resolution passed for this purpose in 1913 had not been honored.

Sites in Unincorporated Areas

One half mile east of old US 287, south of Hicks Road, immediately west of Big Fossil Creek
HICKS FIELD

Hicks Field is one of three fields established by Canadian troops to train aviators for World War I and later taken over by the U.S. Army for flight training. This field was briefly reactivated during World War II by the Air Force.

In 1923, the government built the world's first helium plant here at a cost of five million dollars. The Bureau of Mines took over the plant, from the U.S. Navy, in 1925 and closed it in 1929 for lack of helium.

Mosier Valley Road, between House-Anderson Road and Knapp Road
MOSIER VALLEY SCHOOL

Robert Johnson and his wife, Dilsie, were the first of a group of emancipated slaves to homestead in Mosier Valley. They named the area for the plantation on which both had worked. Given forty acres as a wedding present by their former owner, Lucy Lee, they deeded four as the site of the Mosier Valley School. Texas Historical Marker, 1983.

Highway 26, two-and-a-half miles northeast of Grapevine
THE MISSOURI COLONY

This historic marker commemorates The Missouri Colony, an early settlement created in 1844 and 1845 by related families from Platte County, Missouri. Many of these families remained in the area to build the northeastern section of the county, the first permanently settled part of Tarrant County. Texas Historical Marker, 1979.

Texas Refinery Ranch, fourteen miles southwest on US 377
PATE MUSEUM OF TRANSPORTATION

Begun as a private collection by A. M. Pate, Jr., this museum boasts an array of classic, antique and special interest automobiles and aircraft. Also on exhibit are rockets, a spacecraft, and an antique railroad car, Ellsmere, built in the 1880s for the president of the Wagner Palace Car Company, Dr. William Seward Webb, and his bride, Eliza Osgood Vanderbilt. The car was donated to the Fort Worth Museum of Science and History by the T & P Railroad and later given to the Pate Museum. The museum's collection includes files on special people and events in transportation.

Also located on the grounds is Founders' Chapel, a country church built about 1900 near the Brazos River in Dennis, Texas, and moved to this location and restored in honor of A. M. Pate, Sr., and Carl Wollner, founders of Texas Refinery Corporation.

FM 1220, fifteen miles north of Fort Worth
WAYSIDE SCHOOL

A school on this site in the Dozier Community was begun in 1883 on land donated by W. E. Boswell. The school is now part of the Eagle-Mountain Saginaw District which includes the W. E. Boswell High School, named in honor of the donor of this original site. Texas Historical Marker, 1968.

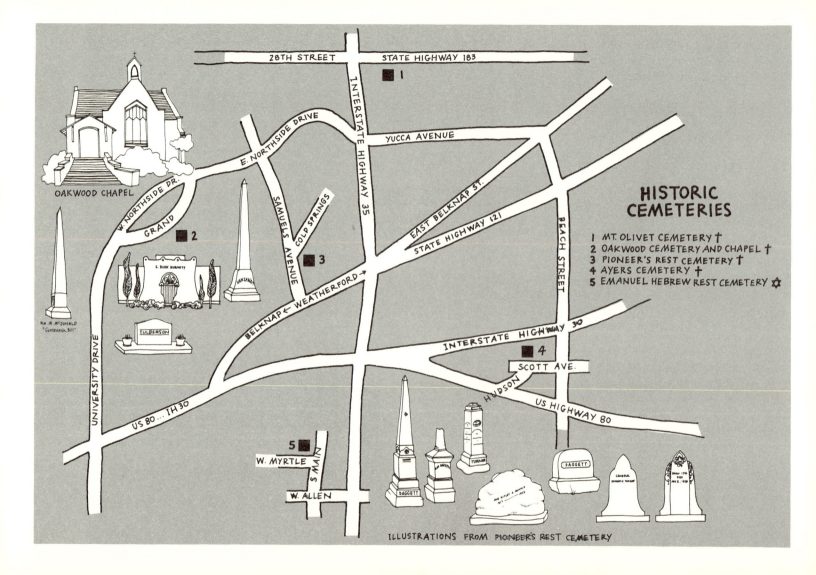

11.

Historic Cemeteries in Tarrant County

Tarrant county has numerous cemeteries of historic interest. Some are still in use today but some have not been used in many years. Often they are maintained by descendents of the original families or by perpetual care societies. Some cemeteries boast elaborately carved headstones and grave markers but in many of these old cemeteries one can still see the cairns of native sandstone which early settlers used to mark graves. In still others, there are homemade grave markers. Unfortunately, many graves are today unmarked, their stones or markers having suffered from exposure and age. The number of tiny graves in many of these cemeteries testifies to the high infant mortality rate in the late nineteenth century.

Cemeteries listed in this section are arranged alphabetically by location—Fort Worth, then suburban communities. However, two cemeteries in Fort Worth of major historical interest are listed first. They are Pioneer's Rest and Oakwood, both on Fort Worth's North Side.

701 Grand Avenue
OAKWOOD CEMETERY AND CHAPEL

In 1879, John Peter Smith, one of the city's first settlers and most prominent civic leaders, gave twenty acres to the city for this cemetery. The cemetery was enlarged to 100 acres. There are actually three cemeteries—Oakwood, Calvary and Trinity—within these boundaries. Plots are owned by lodges, unions and individuals of all races and faiths, and tracts are dedicated to both Union and Confederate soldiers.

A life-sized statue of a Confederate soldier, made of Italian marble, was erected by the United Daughters of the Confederacy in a plot reserved for Confederate soldiers and their wives. The plot reserved for Union soldiers similarly has a bronze marker. Many prominent citizens are buried in Oakwood Cemetery, including John Peter Smith, original donor of the land. (Please see entry under

GOV. CHARLES A CULBERSON
born June 10, 1855
died March 19, 1925

WM. M. McDONALD
"Gooseneck Bill"

Smith, John Peter—Fort Worth, Downtown). Others include:

Euday Louis Bowman—a Fort Worth native and ragtime composer best known for the classic "12th Street Rag." His other songs include "Fort Worth Blues," which was never published.

William A. Bryce—Brick mason who was involved in the building of many large Fort Worth buildings as well as the paving of Camp Bowie Boulevard. Please see entry under Historic Homes—Fort Worth, for the Bryce home. Bryce, a native of Scotland, served as mayor of Fort Worth from 1927 until 1933. He died in 1944.

Belle Burchill—postmistress, appointed in 1881, who started home delivery in Fort Worth. Actively concerned for the welfare of Fort Worth's children, Mrs. Burchill was responsible for establishing a Benevolent Home for the care of destitute or orphaned children. Please see entry for Arnold Park, Fort Worth—North Side.

Samuel Burk Burnett—rancher and oilman. At age 19, Burnett drove herds over the cattle trails. A friend of Quanah Parker and Geronimo, he leased land from the Indians and, in 1900, purchased the 6666 Ranch which later produced vast quantities of oil. He was a founder of the Texas and Southwestern Cattle Raisers Association. The story is told that in the 1890s Burnett, living in a mansion on the present site of the All Church Children's Home, served dinner to Gov. Hogg on an $1800 set of dinnerware. Several generations of Burnetts are also in the family mausoleum. Please see entries for Burk Burnett Building and Burnett Park, Fort Worth—Downtown.

Governor Charles A. Culberson—governor from 1895 until 1899. Culberson previously served two terms as Attorney General of Texas, enforcing the reform policies of Governor James S. Hogg. He succeeded Hogg as governor. Later, Culberson served four terms in the U.S. Senate where he was known for his knowledge of the law.

Captain M. B. Loyd—a Texas Ranger before the Civil War. As agent for a Kansas railroad, Loyd solicited business of cattle drovers who came through Fort Worth and was important to the city's business during the days of the cattle drives. He established the First National Bank and was president of it until his death.

William "Gooseneck Bill" Madison McDonald—active black politician whose ability to unite black and white voters led to his prominence as a leader of the "Black and Tan" faction of the Republication Party in Texas in the early 1900s. McDonald was active in Black Masonic societies, a founder of the Fraternal Bank and Trust Company, and a prominent civic leader.

Winfield Scott—financier, builder, rancher and oilman, Scott came to Tarrant County in 1868. He had a 14,000 acre ranch, was president of the Fort Worth Cotton Oil Company and chairman of the Fort Worth State Bank and built the three-story Metropolitan Building and The Plaza Hotel. (Please see entry for Sundance Square.) Scott also purchased the Waggoner-Wharton home, but died before his family moved into it. (Please see entry for Thistle Hill, Historic Homes—Fort Worth.)

Luke Short—the saloon owner who shot famed Marshal Longhair Jim Courtright (please see story of Courtright-Short gunbattle under Sundance Square). Short returned to Kansas after being "no-billed" for the shooting and died there in 1891 at the age of 39.

W. T. Waggoner—cattleman who drove cattle through the Indian Territory as early as 1869. With Burk Burnett, he leased land from the Indians for grazing. When oil was found on his land, he was disappointed because water was a more urgent need, and he allowed people to carry the oil away in buckets. By 1900, over fifty million barrels had been drilled on his land, making him one of the richest men in Texas. Waggoner moved to Fort Worth in 1905.

Frances Cooke Lipscomb Van Zandt—the mother of K. M. Van Zandt (please see separate entry, under Van Zandt Cottage, Historic Homes—Fort Worth). She was the widow of Isaac Van Zandt, minister from the Republic of Texas to the United States government.

Oakwood Chapel has been aptly called "The Westminster Abbey of Fort Worth" because of its high-pitched ceiling and stained glass windows. It was built in 1912 with funds raised by the sale of cemetery plots. A series of heavy vaults in the lower level were formerly used for the storage of bodies brought from out of town. In the early days, a trap door was used to lower caskets to the waiting horse-drawn hearses. In 1974, the Fort Worth Chapter of Women in Construction led in restoration of the chapel. A new memorial window, honoring J. K. Winston, was installed in 1976. A Texas Historical Marker for the cemetery was placed in 1966; in addition, several graves have markers.

626 Samuels Avenue
PIONEER'S REST CEMETERY

When two of the children of Major Ripley Arnold, commander of the troops at Camp Worth, died in the summer of 1850, his good friend, Dr. Adolphus Gouhenant, allowed burial of the children on his land. Baldwin Samuels gave three more acres in 1871 and, many years later, a cemetery association was formed. Major Ripley Arnold, General Edward H. Tarrant and seventy-five Civil War veterans are buried here. Among the prominent Fort Worth citizens buried here are:

Jules Alvord—trainman for the T&P who was wounded when Sam Bass and his gang robbed the train near Mesquite, Texas, on April 11, 1878. Although wounded, Alvord completed the run instead of seeking medical attention. He died in 1899.

Susan Brown—granddaughter of Daniel Webster. The wife of Louis H. Brown, she died in 1864 at the age of fifty-two.

Brigadier General James J. Byrne—a Union soldier from New York, Byrne was a land agent and surveyor for the T & P and located tracks in the Indian Territory. He was killed in 1880 in an attack on a stagecoach by Indians, led by Apache Chief Victorio, near El Paso.

Ephraim M. Daggett—Veteran of the Mexican War, Daggett was called the Father of Fort Worth in recognition of his contributions to the city's early development. His likeness was engraved on the city seal for the first fifty years of its existence. Daggett's brother and mother, the

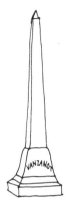

BORN
Queenstown Canada
June 3, 1810
DIED
April 19, 1888

Cemeteries

widow of a Revolutionary soldier, are also buried here.

Carroll M. Peak, M.D.—Dr. Peak was called to Fort Worth from Dallas to minister to Julian Feild (see separate entry under Grist Mill and Saw Mill, Fort Worth—Downtown). Peak liked the people and country well enough to locate here, bringing his bride to a vacated army officer's home in the early 1850s. The first church in Fort Worth was organized in the Peak home. Dr. Peak, a Confederate veteran and mayor of Fort Worth, worked for the first public schools and for the establishment of a railroad in Fort Worth. Mrs. Peak brought the first evergreens to Fort Worth, used for all the weddings and funerals at the time. The Peaks had several children, including Howard, whom local Indians believed had supernatural powers because of his red hair.

General Edward H. Tarrant—Tarrant is said to have served under General Jackson in the Indian campaigns and fought at New Orleans in 1815 and in the Mexican War. He came to Texas in 1835 and immediately entered service as a ranger on the Northwest frontier. Elected to the legislature, he resigned to serve on the frontier and was in command at the Village Creek Battle (please see separate entry, Arlington). Tarrant represented Bowie County at the Annexation Convention and served in the third and fourth legislatures. He was a frequent visitor at the Arnold home in Camp Worth.

"THIS STONE MARKS HIS RESTING PLACE TARRANT COUNTY IS HIS MONUMENT"

Fort Worth—East Side

Ramada Inn Central parking lot, Beach Street at I-30
AYRES CEMETERY

Benjamin Patton Ayres and his wife, Emily, bought a 320-acre farm on this hillside in 1861 and set aside land as a family cemetery. Ayres served as second Tarrant County Clerk when the seat was at Birdville and helped to organize the First Christian Church.

An unknown number of graves, lying outside the fenced family plot, include victims of spring fevers and floods of the Trinity River. The Ayres burial space was reserved when the family sold the property. Texas Historical Marker, 1983.

8550 Meadowbrook Drive
HARRISON CEMETERY

This one-acre cemetery originally belonged to pioneer D. C. Harrison. The earliest grave is dated 1871. Among the other settlers using this site were R. A. Randol, operator of Randol Mill. He bought the land in 1895 and deeded it forever as a burial ground. His first wife, Ronda Harrison, her mother, Nancy Cannon Harrison, and his brother, John C. Randol, who died in an 1894 mill accident, are among the sixty or more people buried here.

Texas Historical Marker, 1982, in memory of Nannie Randol Clark.

Spur 303 (East Rosedale), one block east of Handley Drive
OLD HANDLEY CEMETERY

This spot for a cemetery was chosen over 100 years ago on land owned by the Texas and Pacific Railway Company. The earliest of the 170 marked graves is dated 1878. After 1929, when Rose Hill Cemetery was created, this cemetery began to decline. Texas Electric Service Company keeps the grounds since there are no arrangements for perpetual care.
Texas Historical Marker, 1981.

Fort Worth—North Side

2301 North Sylvania
MOUNT OLIVET CEMETERY

Originally part of the Charles B. Daggett land, this 130-acre cemetery was dedicated in 1907 by F. G. McPeak and was the first endowment care cemetery in the area. It contains statues of a World War I Doughboy and an American GI in honor of veterans. Known for its Memorial Day observance, the cemetery has an Avenue of Flags flown to commemorate days of national and special honor. Each flag was presented by the government to the family of a deceased war veteran and then donated by the family to the cemetery. American Legion Post 628 preserves the Avenue of Flags.

Fort Worth—South Side

South Main Street and Myrtle Street
EMANUEL HEBREW REST CEMETERY

John Peter Smith donated land here in 1879 for use as a cemetery for the city's Jewish residents. The earliest marked grave is that of Leah Kaiser, a child who died in 1879. First maintained by the Emanuel Hebrew Association, the cemetery is now controlled by Congregation Beth-El. The Texas Historical Marker is a gift of Theodore and Ellen F. Mack in memory of Henry Mack, Theodore Mack and Pauline S. Mack.

Members of the Jewish faith were among early settlers in Fort Worth, and the first synagogue was organized about 1892. A new synagogue building was built in 1906 at 819 Taylor Street. The location is now part of the Fritz Lanham Federal Center. Later Congregation Ahavath Sholom (Love of Peace) moved to buildings on 8th Avenue and Myrtle, then to its present location at 4050 South Hulen. In 1902, a portion of the congregation left to organize Congregation Beth-El, with buildings located at 207 West Broadway.

Arlington

2200 Block, North Davis Drive
GIBBINS CEMETERY AND HOMESTEAD SITE

James Gibbins came to Texas from Arkansas in 1857 and bought land near Arlington in 1863. He deeded part of his land to his son, Thomas, who used this family cemetery for the burial of his first wife, Amanda (d. 1877). Thomas's second wife, Martha, maintained the land for three decades after the 1924 death of her husband. The Gibbins family contributed land for a public school and for the Rose-Brown-May Park. Texas Historical Marker, 1982.

621 West Arkansas Lane
MIDDLETON TATE JOHNSON PLANTATION CEMETERY

This cemetery is named for Middleton Tate Johnson, an Alabama native and friend of Andrew Jackson and Sam Houston, who served in the Alabama legislature at the age of twenty-two. In 1865, Johnson served as a delegate to the Texas Reconstruction legislature. Johnson County was named for him in 1854 after his unsuccessful bid for the governorship.

Tomlin Lane (west from North Davis Drive)
TOMLIN CEMETERY

This cemetery was first used in the 1870s by the Wilkinson family, and their graves are marked by clusters of rocks. The oldest grave is that of Solomon Tomlin, a horseman and farmer who brought his family to Texas in the 1860s and who died in 1884. His son, James Tives "Buck" Tomlin, a noted breeder of fine racing horses, bought the cemetery property in 1888. It has been designated to serve descendants of the Tomlin family. Texas Historical Marker, 1982.

1024 North Watson Road, SH 360
P. A. WATSON CEMETERY

Mrs. Micajah Goodwin was buried here in 1846 in a coffin made from the bed of the family wagon. Brush was burned atop her grave to hide it from Indians. There were other graves here when Patrick Alfred Watson of North Carolina bought the land in 1852 and set aside land for this one-acre cemetery. A civic-minded settler, Watson gave land and built Watson Community's first school and church in 1870. In 1950, the Dallas Fort Worth Turnpike was routed around this cemetery. The church, now known as the West Fork Presbyterian Church, was relocated in Grand Prairie. Texas Historical Marker, 1979.

Azle

Northeast corner of Ash and Park Streets
SMITH-FRAZIER CEMETERY

Fort Worth businessman and philanthropist J. J. Jarvis bought land here in 1871 and built a home in the early 1880s. A benefactor to the area's black institutions, he deeded this site as a burial ground for Azle's black community in 1886. There were already several graves here at the time. The site was later inherited by descendants of the Smith and Frazier families. The cemetery is still in use. Texas Historical Marker, 1983.

Bedford

2401 Bedford Road
BEDFORD CEMETERY

The earliest marked grave here is that of Elizabeth White Bobo, a child who died in 1870. The Bobo family had come here in 1870 from Bedford County, Tennessee. In 1877, Milton Moore deeded a five-acre tract, including this cemetery, to New Hope Church of Christ, now Bedford Church of Christ. The Bedford Old Settlers Reunion met here annually for over fifty years. W. L. Hurst, for whom the town of Hurst is named, is buried here (please see entry under Hurst). The cemetery is maintained by the Bedford Cemetery Association. Texas Historical Marker, 1979, sponsored by the First State Bank of Bedford.

Cheek Sparger Road, near the intersection of Jackson Drive
SPRING GARDEN CEMETERY

The burial ground here marks the location of the Spring Garden Community established by the first permanent settler in this area, Samuel Cecil Holiday Witten, in 1854. Witten and Milton Moore built a schoolhouse here and named it for Witten's home in Missouri, Spring Garden. Once the site of churches, a grange and a Justice of the Peace Court, Spring Garden declined in the 1870s after a destructive schoolhouse fire and because population was drawn to the nearby development of Bedford. Texas Historical Marker, 1981.

Colleyville

2700 block of Brown Trail Drive
RILEY CEMETERY

Jonathan Riley, who brought his family to this area from Kentucky, received this land grant in 1863. Legend says that when a thief was killed nearby, Riley gave permission for the first burial here. In 1883, Riley and William Autry set aside this one-acre tract for a graveyard. By then, family and neighbors had also used the cemetery. Riley's descendants left the area before 1890, but the cemetery was used until near the turn of the century. There was one interment during the 1930s. Many graves are now designated only with sandstones, and the rest are unmarked. Texas Historical Marker, 1979.

4700 block of Jackson Road
WITTEN CEMETERY

Samuel Cecil Holiday Witten, a successful landowner, Justice of the Peace and Tarrant County surveyor, came to Texas in 1854. He first used this burial site in 1857 for the interment of his son, William Cecil. His son-in-law, Ryan Harrington, a frontiersman who participated in the 1849 California gold rush, is also buried here. Although Witten and his family moved to Corpus Christi in 1890, the cemetery remained in use by family members. Texas Historical Marker, 1981.

Crowley

300 North Hampton
CROWLEY CEMETERY

Settlers who moved into the Deer Creek area in the late 1840s first used this cemetery. The earliest grave is that of Thomas D. Stephenson, an eight-year-old who died in 1848. The property was deeded for use as a public burial site in 1879 by Sarah J. "Sallie" Dunn. Originally Deer Creek Cemetery, the name was changed in the 1880s, soon after the settlement of Crowley was organized. Texas Historical Marker, 1980.

Euless

1400 block of Minter's Chapel Road
BEAR CREEK CEMETERY

This cemetery was established adjacent to the Bear Creek Missionary Baptist Church. The earliest marked grave is that of Hiram Jackson Farris, an infant who died in 1858. Isham Crowley, a member of the Peters Colony, donated the burial ground to trustees of the church in 1876. Although the congregation later moved to Dallas County and was renamed Western Heights Missionary Baptist Church, Bear Creek Cemetery is still in use. Texas Historical Marker, 1980.

2600 Calloway Cemetery Road
CALLOWAY CEMETERY

The earliest marked graves here are those of two brothers, Richard H. and Joseph W. Calloway, who owned this land in the 1860s. Richard's widow, Catherine, deeded one-and-a-half acres for use as a public burial ground in 1886. The wooden tabernacle was constructed in 1908, and families maintained the grounds until 1971 when a perpetual care fund was established. Texas Historical Marker, 1980, in honor of those who cared for the cemetery.

1000 block of Minter's Chapel Road
ALEXANDER DOBKINS CEMETERY

Alexander Dobkins and his wife, Mary, migrated to Texas from Tennessee in 1852. Ordained as a minister in nearby Bear Creek Baptist Church, Dobkins also served as postmaster for Estill's Station during the Civil War. He died in 1869, and his grave is the earliest marked one on this land which was originally part of his 200-acre farm. Dobkins' son, William C., a physician, businessman and civic leader, is also buried here, along with family members and friends. The cemetery is inaccessible, located on land owned by D/FW Airport. Texas Historical Marker, 1981.

Forest Hill

5713 Forest Hill Drive
FOREST HILL CEMETERY

One of the oldest burial grounds in the county, this cemetery was used for many years before records were kept. Press and Jane Farmer, who lived in this area before the establishment of Camp Worth, are buried here. Few headstones are visible because most graves were unmarked or marked with field stones which have since disappeared. The cemetery is full, however.

Grand Prairie

602 Fountain Parkway (north of parking lot)
FORD CEMETERY

Pinkney Harold Ford and his family migrated from Kentucky to Texas in 1855 and settled in the area of North Arlington then known as the Watson Community. A Civil War veteran, Ford purchased this property in 1879 from John J. Goodwin and designated it as a community burial ground. The earliest marked grave is that of Maria Trayler who died in 1858. Texas Historical Marker, 1981.

North Dooley Street at Wildwood Lane
GRAPEVINE CEMETERY

In 1878, brothers Samuel D. and Allen B. Coble sold four-and-a-half acres of their land here for use as a public cemetery. The earliest grave is that of Louisa C. Guiry who died in 1860 at the age of twenty-two. Pioneer settlers buried here included Barton H. Starr, first mayor of Grapevine, and James Tracy Morehead, second judge of Tarrant County. Additional land south of the original tract was acquired in 1925. Texas Historical Marker, 1980.

West Airfield Drive, one quarter mile north of Glade Road intersection
MINTER'S CHAPEL CEMETERY

Lay Minister Green W. Minter organized Minter's Chapel Methodist Church in 1854. His son-in-law, James Cate, set aside slightly over four acres for a church and a burial ground. The earliest grave is that of A. M. Newton who died in 1857. In 1882, the original log meetinghouse was replaced by a frame structure. D/FW Airport acquired the land in 1967, except for the cemetery, and the church was relocated. Texas Historical Marker, 1979.

Highway 26, one quarter mile southwest of Bethel Road
MORGAN HOOD SURVEY PIONEER CEMETERY

Originally part of the Morgan Hood Survey, this small cemetery has been abandoned for over a century. Its one visible grave is marked by pieces of a sandstone burial cairn. Although no written records remain, the graves may be those of members of the Peters Colony who settled in this area in 1844. Texas Historical Marker, 1983.

Highway 157 (one block north of Hall-Johnson Road)
PARKER MEMORIAL CEMETERY

The first person buried here is thought to be Christina Driskill, mother-in-law of Isaac Green Parker, who owned the land. She died in 1862. In 1881, Parker's widow, Molly, deeded the land for a public burial ground for the Pleasant Glade community. A tabernacle was erected in 1928 and used first for funeral services and later for meetings of the cemetery association. Formerly known as Clements Cemetery, it was renamed in 1937. Texas Historical Marker, 1979.

Haltom City

6100 block of Cemetery Road
BIRDVILLE CEMETERY

The oldest marked grave here belongs to Wiley Wilda Potts who died in 1852. A one-acre tract, then part of the George Akers grant, was legally set aside for burial purposes before 1860. More land was later donated, and by 1910, the site included over three and a quarter acres. It now covers seven acres. The Birdville Cemetery association, organized under a fifty-year charter in 1917, was rechartered in 1967. The cemetery contains over 500 graves, and several families have four generations buried in the family plot. It is still in use today. Texas Historical Marker, 1975.

Judge Benjamin Franklin Barkley is one of the more interesting pioneers buried here. An opponent of slavery, Barkley emancipated the slaves on his Kentucky farm in 1855 and settled in Birdville with his family. A physician, lawyer, charter member of the Fort Worth Masonic Lodge and Republican leader, Barkley spoke out against slavery and secession. Admired for donating land for Birdville's first school, participating in Indian campaigns and supporting Birdville as the county seat, he nonetheless stirred anger and barely escaped death several times because of his strong pro-Union stand.

During the war, Barkley treated wounded Confederate soldiers and aided their families. At this time, he served as local postmaster, but during Reconstruction, he headed the County Registration Board which denied the vote to former Confederate supporters. Appointed County Judge in 1867, he used federal troops to maintain order. With great courage, he conducted a hearing on violent Ku Klux Klan activities. Barkley was defeated when Democrats won all county offices in 1873, but he remained active in law and medicine until his death.

During Reconstruction, Barkley's daughter, Francina Alice, served as postmistress, although only fifteen years old. She was eligible because she had not supported the Confederacy. Her brother, Leonidas "Lon" Barkley, was Postmaster of Fort Worth during the terms of Theodore Roosevelt and William Howard Taft. A Texas Historical Marker commemorating Barkley was placed in 1979.

Hurst

Arwine Cemetery Road
ARWINE CEMETERY

Daniel Arwine, raised in Indiana, began farming in Texas after the Civil War. A Deputy U.S. Marshall, he deeded six acres for a school, church, and cemetery in 1879. The first burial here was his daughter, Katy, who died in 1879. The grave of his uncle, Enoch Sexton who died in 1890, has the oldest stone in the cemetery. Arwine, his wife and parents are among those buried in the 279 marked graves. His descendants and local Boy Scouts maintained the cemetery until the Arwine Cemetery Association was formed in 1975. Texas Historical Marker, 1976.

1400 block of Cardinal Drive
PARKER CEMETERY

Isaac Duke Parker, who donated land for this cemetery in 1901, was the son of Isaac Parker, politician for whom Parker County is named and uncle of Cynthia Ann Parker, the famous Comanche captive. Like his father, Isaac Duke Parker served in the Texas Legislature. Texas Historical Marker, 1968.

Keller

Bourland Road, south of Bancroft Road
BOURLAND CEMETERY

Aurelius Delphus Bourland, a Civil War veteran from North Carolina, bought land here in 1873. A farmer and Baptist preacher, he used this site as a private cemetery for his family. The earliest marked grave belongs to his infant grandson, A. Delphus White, who died in 1886. Bourland sold the site in 1899 for use as a public cemetery for the nearby community of Keller. The red sandstone gateway was constructed by the Works Progress Administration (WPA) in 1935. Texas Historical Marker, 1981.

Bancroft Road, across from Mt. Gilead Church
MT. GILEAD CEMETERY

This burial ground originally served the Peters Colony, a settlement of related families who came from Missouri in the late 1840s. Colony leader, Permelia Allen, who died in 1866, is buried here in an unmarked grave. Her sons-in-law, Daniel Bancroft and Iraneous Neace, first owned the site. The earliest marked grave is that of William Joyce, who died in 1854. Several of the grave markers are homemade. Texas Historical Marker, 1981, placed by Keller State Bank.

Kennedale

New Hope-Hudson and Village Creek Road
SNIDER CEMETERY

This land was used as a burial site by Joel Snider and his family, who moved to Texas from South Carolina in the 1840s and settled here in 1856. The oldest marked grave is that of Daniel McVean, a stonecutter from New York who died in 1858. Snider and his wife are both buried here. Texas Historical Marker, 1982.

Mansfield

FM 917 and Burl Ray Drive
CUMBERLAND PRESBYTERIAN CEMETERY

This site was first used as a burial ground shortly after the Civil War, and the earliest legible gravestone is that of Julia Alice Boisseau Man who died in 1868. She was the wife of Ralph S. Man, co-founder of Mansfield (please see entry for Man Family Homestead in Historic Homes, Mansfield). Other graves hold Civil War veterans and victims of the 1918–19 influenza epidemic. The cemetery was deeded to the Mansfield Congregation of the Cumberland Presbyterian Church in 1874. Texas Historical Marker, 1982, by the Mansfield Cemetery Association.

Newt Patterson Road, four-and-a-half miles northwest of Mansfield
GIBSON CEMETERY

Garrett and James Gibson and their families came to Tarrant County in 1853 and established the Gibson community. Each brother donated land for this cemetery. The earliest marked grave belongs to Garrett Gibson's infant grandson who died in 1866. All but two of the seventy-three marked graves, many of which have only fieldstones, belong to relatives of the Gibson family. Texas Historical Marker, 1983.

Southlake

3100 block of North Carroll Avenue
ABSALOM H. CHIVERS CEMETERY

Absalom H. Chivers, a prosperous farmer and stockman, came here from Mississippi in 1852 and operated a farm along Dove Creek until his death in 1856. His grave is thought to be the earliest in this cemetery which is located on his original homestead. His widow, Eleanor, set the land aside as a family cemetery in 1889. She died in 1896, and her grave is believed to be the last placed in the cemetery. Texas Historical Marker, 1982.

2800 block of Southlake Boulevard
THOMAS EASTER CEMETERY

Thomas Easter, a native of Virginia, settled in Tarrant County about 1848 and patented a 640-acre tract in the northeast corner of the county. He died and was buried here in 1862. His wife, Charity, was buried here in the early 1880s as was Hardin West, a settler who died in 1881. A number of the graves are unmarked. The Easter schoolhouse stood beside the cemetery during the nineteenth century. Texas Historical Marker, 1983.

Peytonville Avenue, one mile north of FM 1709
HOOD CEMETERY

Thomas Hood, a Peters colonist, came from Missouri about 1845 to farm this land. He and his second wife, Maryetta, are buried here in unmarked graves. Several other Peters colonists and Confederate veterans are also buried here. The earliest marked grave is that of Urias Martin, who died in 1855. In 1871, Hood's family formally set aside the one-acre cemetery tract. The cemetery is on privately-owned land. Texas Historical Marker, 1982.

Unincorporated Areas

FM 1220, south of Newark
DIDO CEMETERY

Dempsey S. Holt donated three acres in 1887 for a school, church and cemetery, and Isaac Van Zandt, pioneer physician and Confederate veteran, deeded additional land in 1894. The earliest marked grave is that of Amanda Thurmond, an infant who died in 1879. The village of Dido, named for the mythological queen of Carthage and once a thriving community with a post office and stores, declined after the railroad bypassed it in the 1890s. Texas Historical Marker, 1977.

OAKWOOD CHAPEL

12.

Historic Homes in Tarrant County

Fort Worth

5100 Crestline
THE BALDRIDGE HOUSE

This elegant residence was built in 1910–1913 by Earl and Florence Baldridge on land that was part of the original 1890s development that later became Arlington Heights. Designed by Sanguinet & Staats, the home features massive limestone columns on the facade and carved oak woodwork in the interior. It was occupied for many years by W. C. Stonestreet, a prominent Fort Worth clothier. Texas Historic Landmark, 1978. Modifications were made to the building after the placement of the historic marker.

1730 Sixth Avenue
M. A. BENTON HOUSE

This Victorian gingerbread cottage was erected by pioneer businessman Meredith A. Benton in 1898. At that time, this four-lot site was out in the country, and Mrs. Benton feared living in "the Wild West." The cottage was designed by Benton's father and has a central hall, six rooms, and tiled fireplaces. Mrs. Benton, an active civic worker, helped plant rose beds that are now part of The Botanic Gardens. The Benton family lived here until 1942. Texas Historical Marker, 1971; listed in the National Register of Historic Places.

4900 Bryce
THE WILLIAM A. BRYCE HOUSE

William A. Bryce, a native of Scotland, moved to Fort Worth in 1883 and established a successful brick contracting business. He built this house, designed by Sanguinet & Messer, in 1893. Bryce, mayor of Fort Worth from 1927 to 1933, named the home *Fairview*. A rare example of chateauesque design in Texas, *Fairview* features Richardsonian arches and gabled dormers. Texas Historic Landmark, 1983.

1110 Penn Street
EDDLEMAN-McFARLAND HOUSE

Designed by Howard Messer, this Victorian house was built in 1889 for Sarah C. Ball, widow of Galveston banker George Ball. William H. Eddleman, a local banker, bought the home in 1904 and in 1921 gave it to his daughter, Carrie, the wife of cattleman Frank H. McFarland. The finely crafted interior retains most of the original woodwork and fixtures. The exterior features marble, sandstone, brick and copper.

The house is now owned and occupied by the Fort Worth Junior League. The offices of the Historic Preservation Council for Tarrant County are on the second floor. Texas Historical Marker, 1983; listed in the National Register of Historic Places.

902 South Jennings Avenue
LANERI HOUSE

John B. Laneri, an Italian immigrant, moved to Fort Worth in 1883. A prominent businessman and civic leader, he founded the O. B. Macaroni Company, still in business in the 1980s, and started a private boys' school known as Laneri College. This residence was built in 1904 in one of the city's most prosperous neighborhoods. The brick structure features classical detailing and fine interior woodwork. Laneri occupied the house until his death in 1935. In 1982 it was renovated and remodeled into office space. Texas Historic Landmark, 1982.

EDDLEMAN McFARLAND

University Drive and Colonial Parkway
LOG CABIN VILLAGE

Please see separate entry, Fort Worth—South Side, for information on this collection of authentic restored nineteenth century log cabins.

1120 Penn Street
POLLOCK-CAPPS HOUSE

Built in 1898 for Dr. and Mrs. Joseph R. Pollock, this mansion was sold in 1909 to William Capps and his wife. The family lived here until 1971. The grounds of the house featured a golf course, tennis court, and a three-car garage with a ballroom above. The Pollocks-Capps House was one of several Victorian mansions, homes of bankers, businessmen, cattlemen, lawyers, physicians and publishers, which caused this neighborhood to be called "Quality Hill."

4729 Collinwood
MARSHALL R. SANGUINET HOUSE

Sanguinet, the noted Fort Worth architect, built this shingle style house about 1894 on the site of an earlier home which had burned. Sanguinet was associated with many of the city's early multi-story buildings and with the development of the Arlington Heights subdivision which included his home. Texas Historic Landmark, 1981; listed in the National Register of Historic Places.

POLLOCK-CAPPS HOUSE

600 block, Eighth Avenue
MITCHELL-SCHOONOVER HOME

Completed in 1907, this house was designed by the Fort Worth firm of Sanguinet and Staats for James E. Mitchell, a jeweler who demanded skilled craftsmanship. The property was purchased in 1920 by Dr. Charles B. Simmons who transferred it to his daughter, Maurine, and her husband, Dr. Frank Schoonover. They lived here until 1979. The building now houses the Commerce Savings Bank. Texas Historic Landmark, 1979.

Homes

509 Pennsylvania, at the end of Summit Avenue
THISTLE HILL

Designed by Sanguinet and Staats, this Georgian Revival home was built in 1903 for A. B. Wharton and his bride, Electra Waggoner, daughter of rancher W. T. Waggoner. Electra named the mansion *Thistle Hill.* Cattleman-investor Winfield Scott bought the house in 1911 but died before he moved in. His wife, Elizabeth, lived here until her death in 1938. Occupied by the Girls Service League from 1940 until 1968, the house was purchased in 1976 by "Save The Scott Home, Inc." and now belongs to Texas Heritage, Inc. Foundation. It is open for public tours and can be rented for private and public functions. Restoration is underway, and many of the original features of the grounds, such as the pergola and the tea house, have been restored. Inside, the grand staircase was rebuilt in 1984. Much of the restoration has necessarily involved less obvious repairs such as wiring, plumbing and a new green tile roof, using about eighty percent of the original tiles. Texas Historic Landmark, 1977; listed in the National Register of Historic Places.

2900 Crestline Road
HOME OF K. M. VAN ZANDT

This log house with a clapboard veneer was located on the Weatherford stage line and belonged to civic leader K. M. Van Zandt. Born in Tennessee, he was the son of Isaac Van Zandt, minister from the Republic of Texas who negotiated the annexation of Texas by the Union.

K. M. Van Zandt came to Texas in 1839 and was admitted to the bar in 1858. During the Civil War, he fought with the Texas Infantry, was captured in Tennessee and released at the 1862 exchange of prisoners in Vicksburg. Promoted to the rank of major, he fought with Granbury's brigade and at Missionary Ridge saved the heavy guns of his unit by pushing them by hand when the horses wavered under fire.

Following the war, Van Zandt left East Texas and settled his family in Fort Worth. He established a dry goods store, but soon became active in the oldest banking firm in Fort Worth, Tidball & Wilson. Van Zandt became a partner in the firm which eventually grew into Fort Worth National Bank, today's Texas American Bank/Fort Worth. Van Zandt was influential in the establishment of public schools and was a powerful force in bringing the Texas and Pacific Railroad to Fort Worth. He represented Tarrant County when the Thirteenth Texas Legislature authorized the incorporation of Fort Worth.

The Van Zandt home was restored in 1936 by the Women's Centennial Committee. Texas Historic Landmark, 1963, marking the centennial of the Civil War.

Two granite markers near the Van Zandt home commemorate Van Zandt and Texas Confederate General H. P. Mabry. A native of Georgia, Mabry fought on several fronts for the Confederacy and became something of a legend when spies reported his horsemen in three different spots miles apart on the same day. In one battle, his arm was shattered in a knife fight with seven men who would have captured him as a spy. Later, he was shot three times and taken captive at Iuka, Mississippi. Mabry

refused to sign the parole during the Vicksburg prisoner exchange until a slur on the Confederacy was removed from the document.

Mabry had come to Texas in 1851, and prior to the war, had served as a member of the Texas Legislature from 1856 until 1860. After the war, he was elected District Judge but was removed by radical Reconstruction authorities. He came to Fort Worth in 1879 and practiced law here until his death in 1885. Texas Historical Marker, 1963, marking the Civil War Centennial.

1404 South Adams
GUNHILD WEBER HOUSE

This house built in 1907 shows the influence of the craftsman-bungalow architecture popular in California at the turn of the century. Purchased in 1914 by C. K. Lee, later a Texas State Bar Association president, the house was home to the Lee family for twenty-nine years. They added a porte cochere and one room to the original structure. Mrs. Gunhild Weber, a native of Norway, has owned the home since 1944. Texas Historic Landmark, 1978.

4936 Crestline Road
HENRY W. WILLIAMS HOME

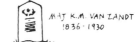

Henry W. Williams, a native of Georgia, was the founder of the H. W. Williams Wholesale Drug Company and a prominent Fort Worth banker. Built for him between 1907 and 1909, this colonial revival style home features an elaborate portico with Corinthian columns and a wide veranda. Williams died in 1925, and the home has since been occupied by several families. Texas Historic Landmark, 1983.

Arlington

211 Willis Street
J. D. COOPER HOME

This colonial home, built in 1878 by J. D. Cooper, has wide board floors and square nails. The home was donated to the City of Arlington by Cooper's son, Horace, and moved to this location from the original site at Abrams and Cooper. It is leased to the Arlington Women's Club. Texas Historical Marker.

Homes

79

1616 West Abram
FIELDER HOUSE

James Park Fielder, a community leader, and his wife built this house in 1914, using steel lathing and other innovative techniques. The brick, prairie-style structure has a large basement for storage of the fruits and vegetables the Fielders grew on the surrounding land. Known as "The Home of the Hill," the Fielder house became the center for social gatherings in the area. For a time, the Ku Klux Klan met in the woods behind the house, and the Dallas-Fort Worth Interurban track ran in front of it.

The home is now owned by the City of Arlington and leased to the Fielder House Foundation, Inc., which operates a museum here. There are two official Texas Historical Markers, one for the building and one describing the Fielders' contributions to Arlington. Both markers were sponsored by the Robert E. B. Fielder family and placed in 1979.

312 North Oak
HUTCHESON-SMITH HOME

The gingerbread trim and general style of this house, built in 1896, reflect the Queen Anne period. The home was built by I. L. Hutcheson, a pioneer Arlington merchant, and purchased in 1919 by the family of S. T. Smith, who lived here until the late 1970s. Texas Historic Landmark, 1982.

621 West Arkansas Lane
JOPLING-MELEAR LOG CABIN

George Washington Jopling built this log cabin in 1863 in the Johnson Station community for his wife and large family. A farmer, cattleman and cotton gin owner, Jopling was a community leader and helped organize the Johnson Station Masonic Lodge. After his wife's death, Jopling deeded the cabin to his daughter and her husband, Z. T. Melear. The cabin was moved to this site in 1970. Texas Historical Subject Marker, 1979.

Ragland Road and Webb-Britton-Arlington Road, seven miles east of the intersection
MARION LOYD HOMESTEAD

Brothers Marion and James Loyd, natives of Arkansas, purchased this land in 1859. Marion, a cattle rancher and civic leader, built a log house here and dug a well that made his home a gathering place for travelers and neighbors. Lloyd descendants have stayed on the land. The log cabin today is covered with a modern exterior. Texas Historical Marker, 1979.

621 West Arkansas Lane
P. A. WATSON LOG HOUSE

Watson built this house in 1855 for his six children, after his first wife died. Remarried in 1858, he had six

Homes

more children, and the house was enlarged. It was occupied by his descendants until 1961 and was moved to this site in 1976. Texas Historical Subject Marker, 1979. Please see separate entry for Watson Cemetery, under Cemeteries, Arlington.

Colleyville

1416 Glade Road
BIDAULT HOUSE

Anthelm Bidault, French farmer and winemaker, built this house of molded concrete blocks. Construction took from 1905 until 1911. Bidault's farm was noted for its orchards, berry fields, and vineyard. During World War I, French soldiers stationed at Camp Bowie received a warm welcome here. The Bidault family returned to France in 1920, but the house is now owned and occupied by a grandson who purchased it many years after it had passed out of the family. Texas Historic Landmark, 1980.

Grapevine

205 Main, Liberty Park
TORIAN LOG CABIN

Of handhewn logs, this cabin was built about four miles from this site, on a creek at the edge of the Cross Timbers (please see separate entry under The Founding of Tarrant County). Located near the community of Dove, it was built by Francis Throop, a Peters colonist from Missouri, and sold first to J.C. Wiley, then to John R. Torian. Torian family members occupied the home until the 1940s. The cabin was moved to this site in 1976. Texas Historic Landmark, 1978.

Mansfield

604 West Broad Street
RALPH MAN HOMESTEAD

Ralph Man, a native of South Carolina, helped found the town of Mansfield with his brother-in-law and business partner, Julian Feild (please see separate entry, Grist Mill and Saw Mill, Fort Worth—Downtown). They operated a steampowered grist mill to supply grain to the Confederacy during the Civil War and later supplied U.S. troops at Fort Belknap and Fort Griffin. The original mill is thought to have been located near the veteran's monument next to the Mansfield City Hall. A marker there commemorates the Feild and Man Grist Mill.

Man built the log portion of this home for his family in 1866 and added the brick rooms later. Texas Historical Subject Marker, 1977. Both names are spelled incorrectly on the marker.

White Settlement

Las Vegas Trail, one block south of White Settlement Road
WILLIAM TERRY ALLEN LOG CABIN

William Allen came to this area from Kentucky as a child and settled on 360 acres at this site in 1857. After serving in the Confederate army, he married and settled on 160 acres, building this thirteen by eighteen cabin in 1864 on a site about six miles west of the Tarrant County Courthouse. It was added to several times and included a Professor's Room, reserved during school months for the local teacher.

The cabin was the family home until 1908 when a frame cottage was built nearby. Allen's heirs sold the property in 1933, and the new owner moved the cabin and enlarged it again. In 1953, the land was purchased for runway additions to Carswell Air Force Base and the cabin moved to Fort Worth. The White Settlement Historical Society raised funds to dismantle the cabin, number the logs, and reconstruct it on its present site. Texas Historical Subject Marker, 1978.

Silver Creek Road, three miles northwest of White Settlement City Hall
TANNAHILL-STUBBS HOMESTEAD

Tannahill, a Scotsman, and his wife came here from Missouri in 1853. In 1856, he patented 320 acres on the Fort Worth-Azle Road and built this house of field stones. Tannahill served as a Tarrant County judge and used the front room for a post office from 1878 to 1885. The house was also the first stagecoach stop west of Fort Worth. It was sold in 1945 to Verna and Johnnie Stubbs, who restored it in 1959. Texas Historic Landmark, 1979, sponsored by the White Settlement Historic Society.

LANERI HOUSE

13.

Historic Houses of Worship

Fort Worth

116 Elm Street
ALLEN CHAPEL AFRICAN METHODIST EPISCOPAL CHURCH

Organized about 1870 by the Rev. Moody, a pioneer circuit rider, and five area settlers, this is the oldest and largest African Methodist Episcopal Church in Fort Worth. The congregational name was adopted in 1879 to honor Richard Allen, a former slave who became the first bishop of the A.M.E. Church. The current sanctuary was designed by William Sidney Pittman, son-in-law of Booker T. Washington. Built between 1912 and 1914, the Tudor-Gothic-Revival building features a tower and stained glass windows. Texas Historical Subject Marker, 1982; Recorded Texas Historic Landmark, 1983.

305 West Broadway
BROADWAY BAPTIST CHURCH

This congregation was organized in 1882, meeting in a rented hall at 15th and Houston Streets. A wooden frame church was built on this site in 1886, and the congregational name became Broadway Baptist Church in 1890. A brick church, built in 1906, was destroyed in the Southside fire of 1909, but a replacement was completed in 1910. The present sanctuary, begun in 1949, was dedicated on Easter Sunday, 1952. In its centennial year, the congregation numbered over 2,500 members. Texas Historical Marker, 1982.

3290 Lackland Road
CHRIST THE KING EPISCOPAL CHURCH

Organized in 1953, the congregation of Christ The King Episcopal Church decided in 1975 to acquire and restore an old country church for its main building. That year, the old Buckner Methodist Church, built in 1907, was moved to Fort Worth from the Buckner community. Cut into sections to be moved, the building was reassembled and extensively renovated, with the bell tower built to its original height and a new steeple added. An organ from a Catholic Church in St. Louis was restored and installed in 1976. The church contains wood carvings from England, antique English chandeliers from a home in Savannah, Georgia, windows from a department store, and antique pews from St. Paul's Methodist Church in San Antonio.

612 Throckmorton
FIRST CHRISTIAN CHURCH OF FORT WORTH

The city's oldest congregation was organized in 1855 by the Rev. A. M. Dean who came to the six-year-old village carrying his hymnbook and revolver. He held services in a log house built as quarters for an officer.

The congregation's first regular meeting place was a one-story concrete house at Lamar and Belknap. A plaque placed by the Tarrant County Historical Society marks the site.

Many noted ministers have preached to this congregation, among them the Rev. Joseph Clark whose sons, Addison and Randolph, founded Add-Ran College, the forerunner of Texas Christian University. Texas Historical Marker, 1970.

1101 Evans
MOUNT ZION BAPTIST CHURCH

The church was organized on Christmas Day, 1894, with five members. The first building, erected in 1907, was located at the corner of Louisiana and Rosedale, and the present site was acquired in 1915. The brick church building was erected in 1919, and an education building was added later. Texas Historical Marker, 1978.

Tenth and Lamar
SAINT ANDREWS EPISCOPAL CHURCH

The first recorded Episcopal service in Fort Worth was held in 1860 by the Bishop of the Diocese of Texas. At that time, a licensed layreader served Episcopalians in both Fort Worth and Birdville. In 1875, the bishop of the newly created jurisdiction of Northern Texas established Saint Andrew's Church with a membership of ten. The name was chosen at the request of a donor from Connecticut who gave money for a church building. The church at this site was built in 1912 and consecrated in 1939. The Chapel and Parish House were also completed and consecrated in 1939. Marker placed by the church.

ST ANDREWS

908 Pennsylvania Avenue
SAINT JOHN'S EVANGELICAL AND REFORMED CHURCH

A United Church of Christ, chartered in 1882, held worship services in a home for twelve families of German descent. The church's original sanctuary was built on Calhoun Street but was moved on wheels to the corner of Texas and Taylor and then relocated again to this site in 1915. Texas Historical Subject Marker, 1982.

509 West Magnolia
SAINT MARY OF THE ASSUMPTION

The fourth Roman Catholic parish in Fort Worth was established in a small wooden structure here in 1909. Despite fire damage to the building in 1918 and again in 1922, the parish grew. The present Romanesque revival structure was designed by the architectural firm of Sanguinet, Staats and Hedrick and dedicated in 1924. Texas Historical Marker, 1979.

1206 Throckmorton
SAINT PATRICK'S CATHEDRAL

Early in the city's history, Catholic mass was celebrated in private homes each spring and fall when a visiting priest rode horseback from San Angelo. The first resident priest arrived in 1875. Three members of the Catholic community pledged security for $300 to be used to purchase land between Tenth and Twelfth for a cathedral, and the cornerstone was laid in 1888. The building was completed in 1892.

The walls of the cathedral are quarried stone. Improvised, horse-powered lathes were used to turn and polish the eighteen interior pillars. The ceilings and window frames are wood-grained, and the stained glass windows were imported from Germany. The bell, cast in Troy, New York, has been in use since 1888. Texas Historic Landmark, 1962.

ST. PATRICK'S CATHEDRAL

1800 West Freeway
ST. PAUL LUTHERAN CHURCH

In the early 1890s, services were conducted in German at the Knights of Honor Hall in downtown Fort Worth. A mission, the Evangelisch Lutherische St. Paulus Gemeinde, was chartered in 1896 and a small chapel erected near Hemphill and present Vickery Avenue. The congregation erected a church on May Street in 1919, but continued growth demanded a larger building, and the church relocated here in 1954. Texas Historical Marker, 1982.

Arlington

300 South Center
FIRST BAPTIST CHURCH OF ARLINGTON

This church was organized in the 1870s at Johnson Station, an early settlement and stagecoach stop. When the T & P built a line through the area, founding Arlington, the church moved to the new town. A sanctuary at Pecan and Abram, built in 1917, burned in 1944, and was replaced by the auditorium at this site. The sanctuary was added in 1959. Texas Historical Marker, 1982.

4201 Little Road (intersection with Pleasant Ridge Road)
TATE SPRINGS BAPTIST CHURCH

Many local churches grew out of worship services conducted at camp meetings on Village Creek. In February, 1882, ten local residents met to organize the Tate Springs Baptist Church. The Jopling schoolhouse, located on land donated by E. C. Tate, served as the first chapel. The church moved to this site in 1895. Texas Historical Marker, 1982.

Azle

300 South Stewart Street
ASH CREEK BAPTIST CHURCH

This church was organized in 1871, with forty-eight charter members. Reverend J. C. Powers preached with a gun beside his Bible, and men in the congregation kept their rifles on their knees in case of Indian attack. A meeting house was erected here in 1891, with brush arbors for summer meetings. In 1965, a new auditorium was built; the original structure is used for a fellowship hall. Texas Historical Marker, 1979, sponsored by the Azle Museum and the Women's Missionary Union of the Ash Creek Baptist Church.

117 Church Street
AZLE CHRISTIAN CHURCH

This congregation grew from worship services conducted in the 1880s on land donated by Dr. Azle Stewart for whom the town was named. The fellowship met under a brush arbor from 1890 until 1893 when the first sanctuary was completed. The church's first youth organization, Christian Endeavor, started about 1904, and its members established the first public library in Azle in the home of one of the young girls. A new church building was erected in 1974. Texas Historical Marker sponsored by the Azle Museum and the Christian Women's Fellowship of the Azle Christian Church.

Bedford

2401 Bedford Road
BEDFORD CHURCH OF CHRIST

Founded about 1874, this congregation was originally called New Hope Church of Christ and met in a meetinghouse on a farm owned by Milton Moore. Moore deeded five acres to the congregation in 1877. In its early years, the church also served as a school. By 1900, the name Bedford Church of Christ was used. In 1958, the congregation gave the original building to a neighboring church and built a brick auditorium. Texas Historical Marker, 1983.

Colleyville

6005 Pleasant Run (off Highway 121)
PLEASANT RUN BAPTIST CHURCH

This congregation first met in a one-room grange hall in the community known as Bransford. Later, they moved to Pleasant Run School, near the site of the present church. Land was given for a church house in 1904, and Sunday school rooms and a sanctuary were added later. Texas Historical Marker, 1978.

Haltom City

3145 Carson Street
BIRDVILLE BAPTIST CHURCH

Organized in 1853, this congregation lapsed in the years between 1856 and 1864. Then, ten members reorganized it as the United Baptist Church at Fossil Creek. The present name was adopted in 1917. Texas Historical Marker, 1971.

3208 Carson Street
BIRDVILLE CHURCH OF CHRIST

This congregation first met in February, 1852 with twelve persons present. Reorganized in 1882, it met in the Birdville school building. Confederate General Richard M. Gano, the well-known evangelist, conducted a revival here in 1900. In 1906, land was acquired from the John McCord family and a frame building erected. After a 1950 fire, this brick auditorium was constructed. Damaged in a 1970 fire, it has been restored. Texas Historical Marker, 1979.

6205 Rusk
WATAUGA PRESBYTERIAN CHURCH

Founded in the 1850s, the Willow Springs Cumberland Presbyterian Church was reorganized in 1867 and renamed in 1885. Texas Historical Marker, 1972.

3145 Carson Street
WEST FORK BAPTIST ASSOCIATION

Formed in October 1855 when representatives of twelve frontier churches met in the Birdville Baptist Church, this association was created to serve area congregations. Membership increased as more settlers entered the area and new churches were established. The association held its last meeting in 1886 when leaders argued for smaller, more localized associations. Many of the groups formed after that time remain active today. Texas Historical Marker, 1983.

Grapevine

4344 Cheek-Sparger Road
MINTER'S CHAPEL METHODIST CHURCH

Four pioneer families established this congregation about 1854, conducting services in a log cabin on land donated by James Cate for the church, a school and a cemetery. The congregational name honors Rev. Green Washington Minter who was instrumental in the founding and early growth of the fellowship. The church was moved here in 1967 when D/FW Regional Airport took over the original site. Texas Historical Marker, 1982.

Hurst

530 Elm Street
ISHAM CHAPEL (United Methodist Church of Hurst)

This congregation organized in 1866 as a Methodist Protestant Church by a small group of people from Georgia. The first pastor was Rev. Marion Isham. The name was changed in 1942 when the congregation moved from Precinct Road to quarters on Harmon Road. The church moved to the present site in 1964. Direct descendants of the charter members are still active in the church. Texas Historical Marker, 1983. The original church building on Precinct Road burned in 1952 and the site is now occupied by a mobile home park.

Keller

350 Loraine Street
FIRST BAPTIST CHURCH OF KELLER

Founded in 1882, this church met first in a schoolhouse and then in the Union Church Building. It was a charter member of the Tarrant County Baptist Association. Texas Historical Marker, 1983.

Bancroft and Ottinger
MT. GILEAD BAPTIST CHURCH

The Mt. Gilead Baptist Church was chartered in 1850 with eight members, including two slaves. Early services were held in homes and a log schoolhouse at this site on land owned by Daniel Bancroft. The church has worshipped at this site continuously, except for a brief period during the late 1870s and early 1880s. Texas Historical Marker, 1981.

Southlake

Lonesome Dove Avenue
LONESOME DOVE BAPTIST CHURCH AND CEMETERY

This church was organized in February 1846 in the home of Charles and Lucinda Throop by twenty-three Baptists. The first building at this site was erected in 1847, and the adjoining cemetery was organized in 1850. The minutes of this church, from 1846 until 1968, are preserved at Southwestern Baptist Theological Seminary. Texas Historical Marker, 1963.

Acknowledgments

THIS BOOK is an expanded and revised version of earlier publications about historical sites in Fort Worth and Tarrant County. The first one, *Down Historical Trails of Fort Worth and Tarrant County* (1949), was written by the Arlington Heights Junior Historians, with the assistance of Dr. Julia Kathryn Garrett and Mary Daggett Lake. *A Guide to Historic Sites in Fort Worth and Tarrant County* (1963) by W. J. Overman was second and was revised, expanded and reprinted four times, most recently in 1975 under the direction of Mrs. Edward R. Hudson. For these two books, members of the society collected information from a variety of sources.

When it became apparent the guide needed updating and revision, the society asked Ruby Schmidt to undertake the effort and provided a small grant to assist in her work. The book committee of the society began intensive work on the project in the fall of 1981.

The major source of material for this present volume was inscriptions on Texas State Historical Markers, a result of the diligent efforts of the Tarrant County Historical Commission and its chairman, Duane Gage. That commission, the most active county commission in the state, generates twenty-five per cent of all historical marker applications in the state. Material from the markers is used here with the gracious permission of both the Tarrant County Historical Commission and the Texas Historical Commission.

The society is indebted to many individuals who collected and verified information. Edwin G. Troutman devoted long and tireless effort to the project, and Bennett Smith read the manuscript with a careful and critical eye and made significant suggestions. Dr. Ron Tyler's assistance has been invaluable throughout the project. Ben Huseman of the staff of the Amon Carter Museum prepared the index.

The society would like to express a final sincere and heartfelt thank you to Dr. Judy Alter, editor of the Texas Christian University Press, who melded the various forms and styles in the original version of the manuscript into this final product. Discrepancies or errors are certain to occur in a project that calls upon the work of so many different individuals and sources, but we have done our best to eliminate them.

Ruby Schmidt, *President, 1983–*
Dr. Edwin G. Troutman, *President, 1981–83*
Frank Goss, *President, 1979–81*

Index

A. Webb Roberts Library, 46
Absalom H. Chivers Cemetery, 73
Acuff, Roy, 28
Adair, Cornelia, 22
Add-Ran Male and Female College, 46, 84
African Methodist Episcopal Church, 83
Airmail, x
Alexander Dobkins Cemetery, 69
All Church Children's Home, 3, 62
Allen, Permelia, 72
Allen, William Terry, 82. See also William Terry Allen Log Cabin
Allen Chapel A.M.E. Church, 83
Alvord, Jules, 63
American Airlines, 33
American Freedom Train, 45
American Land and Investment Company, 39
Amon Carter Field, viii, 48, 55
Amon Carter Museum, 35–36
Amon Carter Square. See Cultural District, The
Amon Carter YMCA Camp, 35
Amon G. Carter Foundation, 23
Amtrak, 14
Anderson, Neil P., 9
Anderson Chapel. See John G. Anderson Chapel
Ann Waggoner Hall, 50
Anne Burnett and Charles Tandy Foundation, 22
Arlington, 2, 51–53, 64, 66, 69, 79–81, 86
Arlington College. See University of Texas at Arlington
Arlington Downs Race Track, 51
Arlington Heights, 39, 75, 77
Arlington State College. See University of Texas at Arlington
Arlington Training School. See University of Texas at Arlington
Arlington Women's Club, 79
Armour, 27
Armstrong, Captain John, 22
Armstrong and Messer, 20. See also Messer, Howard
Army Air Training Center. See Carswell Air Force Base
Arnold, Major Ripley, ix, 2, 3, 31, 40, 63, 64
Arnold Park, 31, 62
Arwine, Daniel, 71
Arwine Cemetery, 71
Ash Creek Baptist Church, 53, 86
Ash Tree, 56
Atelier Building, 9
Athol, 58
Avenue of Flags, 65
Aviation Industry, vii, viii, x, 32–33, 35, 40, 48–49, 55–56, 58
Ayres, Benjamin Patton, 64
Ayres Cemetery, 64
Azle, ix, 53–54, 67, 86–87
Azle Christian Church, 87

Badgero, Wes and Jerry, 31
Baldridge House, 75

91

Barbier. See Frenchman's Well
Barkley, Judge Benjamin Franklin, 71
Barkley, Leonidas "Lon", 71
Barnett, Alva Pearl, 33
Barron, Cadet Robert J., 55
Barron Field, 49, 55–56
Bass, Sam, 12, 63
Bass Brothers Enterprises, Inc., 7
Battle of Village Creek, 51, 64
Baylor University Medical School, Dallas, 16
Bean, Alan, x
Bear Creek Baptist Church, 68, 69
Bear Creek Cemetery, 68
Bedford, 54, 67, 87
Bedford Cemetery, 67
Bedford Church of Christ, 67, 87
Bedford College, 54
Bedford School, 54
Benbrook, 55
Benbrook, James M., 55
Benbrook Lake, 24
Benton, Meridith A., 75
Berachah Home and Cemetery, 53
Bergen, Edgar, 36
Bidault House, 81
Bierstadt, Albert, 36
Big Tree, Chief, 14
Bird, Jonathan, ix, 1
Bird's Fort, ix, 1, 12, 51
Bird's Fort Treaty, 1, 12, 51
Birdville, ix, 1, 33, 57, 64, 70–71, 87–88

Birdville Baptist Church, 87, 88
Birdville Cemetery, 70–71
Birdville Church of Christ, 87–88
Black and Tan Faction of the Republican Party, 62
Blagg, Dennis, 31
Bolger, Ray, 36
Boswell, W. E., 59
Boswell High School, 59
Botanical Garden, 35, 37, 75
Bourland, Aurelius Delphius, 72
Bourland Cemetery, 72
Bowman, Euday, 15, 62
Brenneke and Fay, 17
Briggs, George W., 24
Broadway Baptist Church, 19, 83
Brooks, Dr. W. B., ix
Brown, Lloyd, 20
Brown, Susan (grand-daughter of Daniel Webster), 63
Brown-Lupton Student Center Gallery, 46
Brumbaugh's Furniture, 31
Bryce, William A., 62, 76
Buckner Methodist Church, 84
Buffalo, ix
Bur Oak, 55
Burchill, Mrs. Belle, 31, 62
Burk Burnett Building, 9, 11, 62
Burnett, Samuel Burk, 9, 11, 22, 24, 62
Burnett Park, 11, 62
Burr, George E., 20

Burts, Dr. W. P., ix, 7
Byrne, Brigadier General James J., 63

Calder, Alexander, 11
Calloway Cemetery, 68
Calvary Cemetery, 61
Cameron, General R. A., 20
Camp Bowie, 39–40, 81
Camp Bowie Boulevard, 39, 62
Camp Worth, ix, 2, 3, 31, 57, 63, 64, 69
Cantor, Eddie, 36
Capps, William, 77
Carlisle Military Academy. See University of Texas at Arlington
Carnegie, Andrew, 11
Carswell, Major Horace S., 40
Carswell Air Force Base, x, 40, 48, 49, 82
Carter, Amon G., viii, 35, 38, 48, 50. See also Amon Carter . . .
Caruso, Enrico, 28
Casa Mañana, x, 36
Cassidy, Butch, viii, 5–6, 7
Castle, Captain Vernon and Irene, 55–56
Catholic Church, 85
Cattle, Cattle Drives. See Livestock Industry
Cattleman, The, (magazine), 22
Cattleman's Museum, 22
Cemeteries, xi, 19, 28, 61–74
Central Library, 11

Index

Charles D. Tandy Archaeological Museum, 46
Chisholm, Jesse, 12, 30
Chisholm Trail, vii, 3, 12, 30
Christ the King Episcopal Church, 84
Christian Church, 46, 64, 84
Church of Christ, 87–88
Churches, xi, 19, 46, 50, 53, 64, 66, 67, 68, 69, 70, 72, 74, 83–89
City National Bank Building, 7
City of Fort Worth, 3
Civil War, vii, 19, 32, 40, 50, 53, 54, 56, 57, 62, 63, 69, 71, 72, 78, 81 See also Confederacy (or) Union
Clark, Addison and Randolph, 46, 84
Clark, Rev. Joseph, 84
Clarkson, Wiley G., 23
Clarkson, Wiley, and Paul Cret, 12
Clements Cemetery. See Parker Memorial Cemetery
Cockrell (Hahn), 3
Colleyville, 67–68, 81, 87
Collins, Delia, 31
Comanche Indians, 1, 28, 45, 71. See also Parker, Chief Quanah
Confederacy, vii, 11, 14, 17, 19, 52, 54, 57, 61, 64, 71, 73, 74, 78–79, 81, 82, 87. See also Civil War
Congregation Ahavath Sholom, 65
Congregation Beth-El, 65
Consolidated Vultee Aircraft. See General Dynamics
Continental National Bank, 23
Convair. See General Dynamics
Cooper, J.D., 79
Courthouse, Tarrant County. See Tarrant County Courthouse
Courthouse Square, ix, 17. See also Tarrant County Courthouse
Courtright, Jim, viii, 6–7, 62–63
Cowtown Coliseum, 28
Crimson Limited Express, 49
Crowley, 68
Crowley Cemetery, 68
Culberson, Governor Charles A., 62
Cultural District, The, xi, 35–38, 48
Cumberland Presbyterian Cemetery, Mansfield, 72
Cumberland Presbyterian Church, 72, 88

D/FW International Airport, x, 48, 49, 55, 56, 69, 70
Daggett, Captain Ephraim M., 15, 63
Daggett, Charles B., 65
Daggett, Henry Clay, 33
Dallas, ix, x, 13, 15, 16, 18, 19, 48, 55
Dallas Fort Worth International Airport. See D/FW Airport
Dallas Herald, 18
Darnell, Nicholas Henry, 18

Dean, Rev. A. M., 84
Deer Creek, 68
Delaware Hotel. See Pickwick Hotel
Democrat. See Fort Worth Democrat
Dempsey, Jack, 15
Dempsey-Tunney Fight, 15
Depot, ix. See also Gulf, Colorado & Santa Fe Depot
Dido, 74
Dido Cemetery, 74
Dillow, S. S., 50
Dingee, Arthur S., 23
Dobkins, Alexander, 69
Dobkins, William C., 69
Doug Russell Park, Arlington, 53
Dove, 81
Dozier Community, 59
Drag Stone, 13, 40
Driskell, Earle C., 58
Dunnville, 56

Eagle Mountain Lake, 24, 54
Eagle, The, 11
Eakins, Thomas, 37
Eastern Cattle Trail, vii, 12, 27, 30
Eastern Cross Timbers, 1, 2, 81
Eddleman, William H., 76
Eddleman-McFarland House, 76
Edna Gladney Home, 43
Edrington, W. R., 9
Eisenhower, President Dwight D., 14, 30

El Paso Hotel. See Pickwick Hotel
Electric lights, ix
Elgin National Watch Company
  Band, 20
Elizabeth Boulevard, 43–44, 49
Ellis Pecan Company. See Ku Klux
  Klan Building
Ellsmere, 59
Emanuel Hebrew Association, 65
Emanuel Hebrew Rest Cemetery, 65
Emery, Frances Daisy, 16
Estill's Station, 69
Euless, 55, 68–69
Evangelical and Reformed
  Church, 85
Evatt, William, 54
Everman, 55–56

F. Howard Walsh Foundation. See
  Walsh, F.
Fairview, 76
Farmer, Press and Jane, 69
Farrington Field, 36
Fat Stock Show, ix, 28. See also
  Southwestern Exposition and Fat
  Stock Show
Feathertail, Chief, 3
Federal Courthouse, 12
Feild, Julian, 13–14, 17, 64, 81
Ferguson, Governor Ma, 32
Fielder, James Park, 80
Fielder House, 80

Fire Department, viii, 7–8, 17,
  18–19
Fire Station No. 1, 7–8
First Baptist Church of Arlington, 86
First Baptist Church of Keller, 89
First Christian Church of Fort
  Worth, 64, 84
Flatiron Building, 12–13
Fleming, William, 41
Florence School, 57
Florence Shuman Hall, 47
Ford, Pinkney Harold, 69
Ford Cemetery, 69
Forest Hill, 69
Forest Hill Cemetery, 69
Forest Park Zoo, 44
Fort Worth, vii–xi, 1–50, 55, 56,
  61–65, 66, 71, 75–79, 81, 82,
  83–86
Fort Worth & Denver Railway, 20
Fort Worth—Downtown, vii, viii, xi,
  3, 5–9, 9–25, 27, 28, 30, 64, 81
Fort Worth—East Side, xi, 48–50,
  64–65
Fort Worth—North Side, xi, 31–33,
  48, 49, 65
Fort Worth—South Side, xi, 43–47,
  49, 65, 77
Fort Worth—West Side, xi, 39–41,
  48, 49
Fort Worth Airport. See Meacham
  Field

Fort Worth Art League, 37
Fort Worth Art Museum, 37
Fort Worth Belt (Fort Worth Stock-
  yards Belt Railway), 27
Fort Worth Benevolent Home Asso-
  ciation, 31
Fort Worth Botanical Garden. See
  Botanical Garden
Fort Worth Club, 35
Fort Worth Cotton Oil Company, 62
Fort Worth Democrat, 7, 17
Fort Worth Dressed Meat and Pack-
  ing Company, 27
Fort Worth Independent School Dis-
  trict, 36
Fort Worth Interpretive Center, 7, 8
Fort Worth Junior League, 76
Fort Worth Medical College, 13, 16
Fort Worth National Bank. See Texas
  American Bank
Fort Worth Packing Company, 27
Fort Worth Panthers or Cats, 32
Fort Worth Star-Telegram, 35
Fort Worth State Bank, 62
Fort Worth Stockyards' Company,
  28–29
Fort Worth Theatre, 37
Fort Worth University, 16
Founder's Chapel, 59
Frank Leslie's Illustrated
  Newspaper, 20
Fraternal Bank and Trust Company, 62

Frenchman's Well, 13, 21
Frerichs, Heinrich, 47
Frontier Days, x, 36
Fry Home. See W.T. Fry Home

Gainsborough, Thomas, 37
Gano, General Richard M., 87–88
Garrett, Jenkins, 57
Gas lighting, ix, 19, 24
General Dynamics, x, 35
Geronimo, 62
Ghormley, Grant, 8
Gibbins Cemetery, 66
Gibson Cemetery, Mansfield, 73
Gladney, Edna, 43
Glassco, Daniel, 54
Glassco School, 54
Golden Goddess, 24, 30
Goodnight, Charles, 22
Gouhenant, Dr. Adolphus, 63
Gounoah. See Frenchman's Well
Goya, Francisco, 37
Grand Prairie, 1, 2, 66, 69–70
Grapevine, 56, 69, 81, 88
Grapevine Cemetery, 69
Grapevine Lake. See Lake Grapevine
Grapevine Springs, 12
Grapevine Sun, The, 56
Greater Southwest International Airport. See Amon Carter Field
Green Glade, 57
Grist Mill and Saw Mill. See Mills
Grubbs Vocational College. See University of Texas at Arlington
Grunewald, Peter, 31
Grunewald Pavilion and Amusement Park, 31–32
Gulf, Colorado and Santa Fe Depot, 14, 19. See also Depot
Gunhild Weber House, 79
Gunn and Curtis, 21

Haggart and Sanguinet, 16
Hahn. See Cockrell
Hallaran, Lloyd F., 23
Haltom City, 57, 70–71, 87–88
Hamleton, William, 54
Hammond, L. M., 53
Handley Cemetery. See Old Handley Cemetery
Handley Depot, 49
Handley Power Plant, 49
Handley Station, 49
Harnett, William Michael, 36
Harrington, Ryan, 68
Harris Methodist Hospital, 35
Harrison Cemetery, 64
Hayne, Alfred S., viii, 20
Hedrick, Wyatt C., 17, 22
Helium plant, 58
Hell's Half Acre, viii, 5, 23, 31, 46
Henry W. Williams House, 79
Heritage Park Plaza, 14–15
Hermann Verein (Society) Park, 32
Hicks Field, 49, 55, 58
Hilton Hotel, 8

Hinckley, Herbert M., 38
Historic Preservation Council for Tarrant County, 76
Historic homes, xi, 39, 43–44, 45, 47, 75–82
Hogg, Governor James S., 62
Holly Plant, 23–24
Hood Cemetery, 73
Hope, Bob, 28
Horse Fountain, 15
Horse racing, 51
Hotel Texas. See Hyatt Regency Hotel
Houston, Sam, 12, 52
Hurst, 57, 67, 71, 88
Hurst, William Letchworth, 57, 67
Hutcheson-Smith House, 80
Hyatt Regency Hotel, 15, 35
Hyde Park, 15–16

Ida Saunders Hall, 47
Indian battle, ix, 2–3
Indians, ix, 1, 2–3, 12, 13, 14, 24, 32, 51, 53, 54, 62, 63, 64, 66, 71, 86. See also Parker, Quanah
Inness, George, 37
Integration, x
Interurban, Dallas-Fort Worth, 49, 80
Isham Chapel (United Methodist Church of Hurst), 88

J. D. Cooper House, 79

J. E. Foust & Son Funeral
  Directors, 56
Jacob Snively Expedition, 1
James, Harry, 28
Japanese Garden, 37
Jarvis, J. J., 11
Jennings, Sarah J., 11, 15–16
Jennings, Thomas J., 15–16
Jim Ned, Chief. See Ned, Chief Jim
John G. Anderson Chapel, 50
John Peter Smith Hospital, 19
Johnson, President Lyndon B., 14
Johnson, Middleton Tate, 2, 52, 66
Johnson, Philip, 23, 36
Johnson, Philip, and John
  Burgee, 23
Johnson, Robert and Dilsie, 58
Johnson's Station, 52, 80, 86
Jopling, George Washington, 80
Jopling-Melear Log Cabin, 52, 80
Junior Woman's Building, 47

KXAS-TV, 50
Kahn, Louis I., 37
Katy Lake, 45
Katy Railroad, 45
Keeling, James E., 56
Keller, 58, 72, 89
Keller, John C., 58
Kennedale, 72
Kennedy, President John F., x, 15
Kimbell Art Museum, 37

King, Captain Richard, 22
King, Wayne, 36
Kiowa Raid on Walnut Creek, 54
Knights of Honor Hall, 86
Knights of Pythias Castle Hall, 7, 8
Ku Klux Klan, 32, 71, 80
Ku Klux Klan Building, 32

La Grave Field, 32
Lake Arlington, 49
Lake Como, 39
Lake Erie, 49
Lake Grapevine, 56
Lake Worth, 24
Land Title Office Building, 16
Laneri, John B., 76
Laneri College, 76
Laneri House, 76
Large, Ada (Mrs. B. M.
  Mustard), 20
Last Supper Tableau, 41
Lee, Lucy, 58
Lee, Robert E., 14
Leonard, Archibald, 33, 49–50
Leonard Brothers, (Marvin and
  O. P.), 21
Leonard's Department Store, 21
Library, public, 9, 11, 54
Life of America Building, 24
Lighting. See gas or electric
Lindbergh, Charles, 32
Livestock Commission, 28

Livestock Exchange, 28–29
Livestock Industry, vii, viii, ix, x, 3,
  12, 15, 17, 22, 23, 27, 28–30, 38,
  62, 63, 76, 78, 80
Livestock Marketing Association, 28
Locomotive. See Old 610
  Locomotive
Log Cabin Village, 45, 77
Logan's Run, 23
Lonesome Dove Baptist Church and
  Cemetery, 89
Longbaugh, Harry. See Sundance
  Kid
Lovell, Cora, 54
Lowe, Jim. See Cassidy, Butch
Loyd, Captain M. B., 62
Loyd, Marion, 80
Lusk, John R., 32, 46

M. & O. Express, 21
M. G. Ellis Elementary School, 33
Mabry, General H. P., 78–79
Mail, ix, 14, 17, 52, 62, 69, 71
Malone, Jim, 31
Man, Ralph S., 14, 72, 81
Mansfield, 14, 58, 72, 81
Margaret Meacham Hall, 47
Marine Creek, ix, 27, 29
Marion Loyd Homestead, 80
Marrow Bone Spring, 52
Marshall R. Sanguinet House, 77
Masonic Home and School of Texas, 45

Masonic Temple, 16
Masonry and Masons, 2, 16, 45, 62, 71, 80
Masterson, Bat, 7
Matisse, Henri, 11
Maverick Hotel, 29
McBrayer, Stanley T., 8
McCarthy, Charlie, 36
McCoy Trail, 12
McCrory's variety store, 19
McDonald, William "Gooseneck Bill" Madison, 62
McFarland, Frank H., 76
McPherson, Aimee Semple, 15
Meacham, Henry C., 32
Meacham Field, 32–33, 48, 49
Mechau, Frank, 12
Medical College. See Fort Worth Medical College
Memorial Shaft, 17
Messer, Howard, 20, 76. See also Sanguinet & Messer
Metropolitan Building, 62
Mexican War, 2, 14, 40, 63, 64
Middleton Tate Johnson Plantation Cemetery, 52, 66
Miller, Alfred Jacob, 36
Mills, 13–14, 49–50, 64, 81
Minter, Green W., 70, 88
Minter's Chapel Cemetery, 70
Minter's Chapel Methodist Church, 70, 88

Miranda, 55
Missouri Colony, 59. See also Peters Colony
Mitchell, James E., 77
Mitchell-Schoonover House, 77
Monet, Claude, 37
Moody, Rev., 83
Moore, Henry, 36
Moore, Milton, 54, 67, 87
Moore, W.M. See Junior Woman's Building
Moran, Thomas, 35
Morehead, James Tracy, 69
Morgan Hood Survey Pioneer Cemetery, 70
Morris, Rev. Isaac Z. T., 43
Mosier Valley School, 58
Moudy Building Exhibition Space, 46
Mount Olivet Cemetery, 65
Mount Zion Baptist Church, 84
Mt. Gilead Baptist Church, 89
Mt. Gilead Cemetery, 72
Museum of Science and History. See Fort Worth Museum of Science and History
Museums, 35–36, 37–38, 41, 45, 46, 59
Mustard, Mrs. B. M., 20

Narrow Gauge Railway, 52
Navarro County, 1

Ned, Chief Jim, 2, 3
Neil P. Anderson Building, 9
New Hope Church of Christ. See Bedford Church of Christ
Newby, Mrs. Etta O., 47. See also William G. Newby Memorial Building
Newspaper, viii, 7, 17, 35, 56, 58
Niles, Louville Veranus, 27
Niles City, 27–28
Noble Planetarium, 37
North Fort Worth High School, 33
North Side Public School, 33
Northern Texas Traction Company, 49

O'Bar, 54
O. B. Macaroni Company, 76
Oakwood Cemetery and Chapel, 7, 11, 20, 61–63
Offset printing press, 8
Oil Industry, vii, viii, x, 24, 35, 41, 59, 62, 63
Old 610 Locomotive, 19, 45
Old Handley Cemetery, 65
Omni Theater, 38
Oneal-Sells Hall, 50
Oxford, Zena Keeling, 56

P. A. Watson Cemetery, 66, 81
P. A. Watson Log House, 52, 80–81
Packing houses, vii, ix, x, 27. See also

Livestock Industry
Paddock, Buckley Boardman, viii, 7, 17
Paddock Park, 17
Paddock Viaduct, 17
Panther City, 7–8, 18, 32
Parker, Cynthia Ann, 45, 71
Parker, Elsie Gipson, 54
Parker, George Leroy. See Cassidy, Butch
Parker, Isaac, 45, 71
Parker, Isaac Duke, 71
Parker, Isaac Green, 70
Parker, Quanah, viii, 24, 28, 62
Parker, Robert Leroy. See Cassidy, Butch
Parker Cemetery, Hurst, 71
Parker Memorial Cemetery, Grand Prairie, 70
Pate, A. M., Jr., 59
Pate Museum of Transportation, 59
Peak, Dr. Carroll M., 13, 64
Peters Colony, 68, 70, 72, 73, 81. See also Missouri Colony
Picasso, Pablo, 37
Pickwick Hotel, 24
Pioneer's Rest Cemetery, 61, 63–64
Pittman, William Sidney, 83
Place, Etta, 5–6
Planetarium. See Noble Planetarium
Plaza Hotel, 7, 62
Pleasant Run Baptist Church, 87

Pollock, Dr. and Mrs. Joseph R., 77
Pollock-Capps House, 77
Poly, 50
Polytechnic College, 50
Porter, Fannie, 5
Post, Wiley, 32
Post Office, 17, 52. See also Mail
Post Office, Azle, 54
Presley, Elvis, 28
Probst Construction of Chicago, 21
Prohibition, x
Public Market Building, 18
Public Schools, ix, x, 19, 33, 36, 52, 53, 58, 59, 78

"Quality Hill", 77

Railroad Day, 18
Railroads, vii, viii, ix, 7, 11, 14, 17, 18–19, 20, 21, 22, 25, 28, 45, 55, 57, 58, 59, 63, 74, 78
Ralph Man Homestead, 14, 81
Rand, Sally, 36
Randol, R.A. (Bob), 50, 64
Randol Mill, 49–50, 64
Rathbone, Justus H., 8
Rattikin Title Company, 23
Rauschenberg, Robert, 37
Ray, Martha, 36
Reconstruction, 41, 71, 79
Rembrandt van Rijn, 37
Remington, Frederic, 7, 35

Reno, Jim, 22
Republic of Texas, 51, 52, 63, 78
Republican Party, 62, 71
Reynolds, J. G., 53
Reynolds, Sir Joshua, 37
Richardson, Sid W., 7
Riley Cemetery, 67
Robbins, Reg, 32
Robertson's Collection, UTA, 53
Rock Island Railroad, 57
Rodeo, 28, 51. See also Southwestern Exposition and Fat Stock Show
Rodgers, C. P. "Daredevil Cal", 43–44
Rogers, Will, 32, 35, 38
Roosevelt, President Franklin D., 14, 35, 36
Roosevelt, President Theodore, ix, 28, 71
Rose, Billy, 36
Rose Hill Cemetery, 65
Rubens, Peter Paul, 37
Russell, Charles M., 7, 35
Ryan, John C., 43–44

S. H. Kress and Company, 19
Saint Andrews Episcopal Church, 84
Saint John's Evangelical and Reformed Church, 85
Saint Mary of the Assumption, 85
Saint Patrick's Cathedral, 19, 85

Saint Paul's Lutheran Church, 86
Sanguinet, Marshall R., 7, 8, 12, 16, 75, 76, 77, 78
Sanguinet & Messer, 76
Sanguinet and Staats, 7, 8, 12, 75, 77, 78. See also Haggart and Sanguinet
Santa Fe Railway, 13
Satank, Chief, 54
Satanta, Chief, 54
Saunders, Dr. Bacon, 13
Saunders, T. B., 27, 29
Saunders II, Thomas B., 29
Saunders III, Thomas B., 29
Saunders family, 27, 29
Saunders Hall. See Ida Saunders Hall
Saunders Park, 27, 29
Schoonover, Dr. Frank, 77
Scott, William Edrington, 37, 47
Scott, Winfield, 7, 62, 78
Sears-Roebuck Company, 45
Sellors, Evaline, 20, 36
Seminary South, 45
Shelton, Anna, 47
Shelton, John M., 19
Shelton Building, 19
Short, Luke, viii, 6–7, 62–63
Shriners, 16
Sibley's Brigade, 19
Sid Richardson Collection of Western Art, 7
"Silver Slipper Row", 43

Sinclair Building, 24
Six Flags Over Texas, 52
Smith, John Peter, 11, 15, 19, 61–62
Smith-Frazier Cemetery, 67
Snider Cemetery, 72
Snively Expedition. See Jacob Snively Expedition
Sons of Hermann, Order of the, 32
Southern Baptist Convention, 46
Southlake, 73, 89
Southside Fire of 1909, viii, 18–19, 83
Southwestern Baptist Theological Seminary, 45–46, 89
Southwestern Exposition and Fat Stock Show, 29, 38. See also Fat Stock Show
Southwestern Telephone and Telegraph Company, 22
Southwestern Theological Seminary. See Southwestern Baptist Theological Seminary
Spaghetti Warehouse, 24, 30
Spring Garden Cemetery, 67
Spring Garden Community, 67
Spring Palace, viii, ix, 20
Stagecoaches, ix, 15, 78, 82, 86
Star-Telegram. See Fort Worth Star-Telegram
Starr, Barton H., 69
Steel, Lawrence W., 15

Steiner, Dr. Joseph M., 2
Stewart, Dr. Azle, 87
Stock Show. See Southwestern Exposition and Stock Show
Stockyards Historical District, vii, 24, 27–30
Stonestreet, W. C., 75
Streetcars, ix, 19, 39
Stubbs. See Tannahill-Stubbs Homestead
Sundance Kid (Harry Longbaugh), viii, 5–6, 7
Sundance Square, vii, viii, x, xi, 5–7, 8, 23, 63
Sunday, Billy, 28
Swift and Company, x, 27
Sycamore Creek, 18

Taliaferro Field No. 2. See Barron Field
Tandy, Anne, 11, 22
Tandy, Charles David, 11, 17, 22
Tandy Center Subway, 21
Tannahill-Stubbs Homestead, 82
Tarrant, General Edward H., 1, 51, 63, 64
Tarrant County, founding of and early history, vii–viii, 1–3
Tarrant County Baptist Association, 89
Tarrant County Construction Company, 18

Tarrant County Convention Center, 21
Tarrant County Courthouse, 7, 21, 57, 82
Tarrant County Criminal Courts Building, 3
Tarrant County Junior College, 57
Tarrant Field. See Carswell Air Force Base
Tate Springs Baptist Church, 86
Telegraph, ix
Telephone, ix
Telephone Exchange, 22
Terrell, Ed, 32, 46
Terrell, General George W., 1
Terry Springs, 31
Texas A & M College, 53
Texas Air Transport, 33
Texas American Bank/Fort Worth, 11, 78
Texas and Pacific Railroad, 18, 19, 20, 25, 49, 55, 58, 59, 63, 65, 78, 86
Texas and Pacific Railroad Terminal Building, 19, 22
Texas and Pacific Warehouse, 22
Texas Centennial, x, 36
Texas Children's Home and Aid Society, 43
Texas Christian University, 16, 46, 84
Texas Electric Service Company (TESCO), 14, 32, 49, 65
Texas Heritage, Inc. Foundation, 78
Texas Rangers, 6, 12, 41, 62
Texas and Southwestern Cattle Raisers Association, 22, 23, 28–29, 30, 62
Texas Spring Palace. See Spring Palace
Texas State Teachers Association, 23
Texas Street Central Fire Station, 8
Texas Wesleyan College, 50
Theater organ, 36
Theaters, 36, 37, 38
36th Division, 39
Thistle Hill, 7, 62, 78
Thomas Easter Cemetery, 73
Thorp Spring, 46
Tidball, Thomas A., 11
Tidball & Wilson, 11, 78
Tomlin Cemetery, 66
Torian Log Cabin, 81
Trader's Oak, 32, 33, 46
Trader's Village, 2
Trimble, W. M., 53
Trinity Cemetery, 61
Trinity Forks, 2, 14
Trinity River, vii, ix, 2, 3, 11, 12, 13, 14, 17, 21, 23–24, 32, 51, 64
Truman, President Harry S., 50
Turner & Dingee, 23
Turner and McClure. See Turner & Dingee

Turner Oak, 41
Turner, Charles, 41

U.S. Army, 39, 58
U.S. Navy, 58
U.S. Air Force, x, 40, 58
Union Church Building, 89
Union, 55, 61, 63, 71. See also Civil War
United Church of Christ, 85
University of Texas at Arlington, 53

Valentino, Rudolph, 15
Van Zandt, Frances Cooke Lipscomb, 63
Van Zandt, Isaac, 63, 74, 78
Van Zandt, K. M., viii, 11, 17, 40, 63, 78
Village Creek, 86. See also Battle of Village Creek

W. T. Waggoner Building, 23, 24
W. T. Fry home, 44
WBAP Radio, 50
WBAP–TV, 50
Waggoner, Dan, 50
Waggoner, Electra, 38, 78
Waggoner, W. T., 23, 24, 51, 63, 78. See also W. T. Waggoner Building
Waggoner Library, 22
Waggoner-Wharton home, 62, 78
Wall, Benjamin R., 56

Walnut Creek, 54
Walsh, Mrs. F. Howard, 41
Walsh family, F. Howard, 36, 41
Warhol, Andy, 37
Warren Wagon-Train Raid, 14
Watauga Presbyterian Church, 88
Water Garden, 23
Water Works, 19, 23–24
Watson, Patrick Alfred, 52, 66, 80–81
Watson Community, 66, 69
Wayside School, 59
Welk, Lawrence, 15
West Fork Baptist Association, 88
West Fork of the Trinity, 24
West Fork Presbyterian Church, 66
Westbrook Hotel, viii, 24, 28, 30
Western Company Museum, 41
Western Union Office, 28
Wetmore, Louis, 13, 40

Wharton, A. B., 78
"Where The West Begins", 1, 3
White Elephant Saloon, 6
White Settlement, 82
Wild Bunch, 5
Will Rogers Memorial Coliseum and Auditorium, 38
Willard, Jess, 28
William Edrington Scott Theatre, 37
William G. Newby Memorial Building, 47
William A. Bryce House, 76
William Terry Allen Log Cabin, 82
Williams, Henry W., 79
Willow Springs Cumberland Presbyterian Church, 88
Wills, Bob, 28
Wilson, John B., 11
Winfield's '08, 7
Witten, Samuel Cecil Holiday, 67, 68

Witten Cemetery, 68
Woman's Club of Fort Worth, 47
Wood, H. W., 58
Works Progress Administration (WPA), 72
World War I, viii, x, 8, 15, 17, 39, 55–56, 58, 81
World War II, viii, x, 17, 24, 32, 40, 58
Worth, General William Jenkins, 2, 38
Worth Theater, 36

"Ye Arlington Inn", 39
Yellow Bear, 24

Zane-Cetti, J. S., 25
Zane-Cetti Building, 25

Index